Elements of the College Experience that Foster Leadership Development

William Vasbinder

Elements of the College Experience that Foster Leadership Development

Student and Faculty Perceptions of Elements of the College Experience that Foster Students' Leadership Development

LAP LAMBERT Academic Publishing

Impressum / Imprint
Bibliografische Information der Deutschen Nationalbibliothek: Die Deutsche Nationalbibliothek verzeichnet diese Publikation in der Deutschen Nationalbibliografie; detaillierte bibliografische Daten sind im Internet über http://dnb.d-nb.de abrufbar.
Alle in diesem Buch genannten Marken und Produktnamen unterliegen warenzeichen-, marken- oder patentrechtlichem Schutz bzw. sind Warenzeichen oder eingetragene Warenzeichen der jeweiligen Inhaber. Die Wiedergabe von Marken, Produktnamen, Gebrauchsnamen, Handelsnamen, Warenbezeichnungen u.s.w. in diesem Werk berechtigt auch ohne besondere Kennzeichnung nicht zu der Annahme, dass solche Namen im Sinne der Warenzeichen- und Markenschutzgesetzgebung als frei zu betrachten wären und daher von jedermann benutzt werden dürften.

Bibliographic information published by the Deutsche Nationalbibliothek: The Deutsche Nationalbibliothek lists this publication in the Deutsche Nationalbibliografie; detailed bibliographic data are available in the Internet at http://dnb.d-nb.de.
Any brand names and product names mentioned in this book are subject to trademark, brand or patent protection and are trademarks or registered trademarks of their respective holders. The use of brand names, product names, common names, trade names, product descriptions etc. even without a particular marking in this works is in no way to be construed to mean that such names may be regarded as unrestricted in respect of trademark and brand protection legislation and could thus be used by anyone.

Coverbild / Cover image: www.ingimage.com

Verlag / Publisher:
LAP LAMBERT Academic Publishing
ist ein Imprint der / is a trademark of
AV Akademikerverlag GmbH & Co. KG
Heinrich-Böcking-Str. 6-8, 66121 Saarbrücken, Deutschland / Germany
Email: info@lap-publishing.com

Herstellung: siehe letzte Seite /
Printed at: see last page
ISBN: 978-3-659-29200-2

Zugl. / Approved by: Hartford, University of Hartford, 2012

Dedication

I dedicate this dissertation to my wife Anne. Without her unwavering love, support, and inexhaustible patience I could not have completed this academic journey.

Student and Faculty Perceptions of Elements of the College Experience that

Foster Students' Leadership Development:

A Case Study

William K. Vasbinder

University of Hartford

Dissertation Advisor: Donn Weinholtz Ph.D.

Table of Contents

Leadership Development 1

Chapter 1: Introduction to the Study
Introduction

The intent of this single case study is to determine what elements of a four-year business program's academic preparation help first time job seekers meet employers' expectations for leadership abilities. This study seeks to reveal these elements by examining the self-reported leadership behaviors of students along with faculty interviews at a four-year college in a northeastern state. More specifically, the *Student Leadership Practices Inventory* (Kouzes & Posner, 2002), or S-LPI, along with additional interview questions, was administered to students enrolled in the final year of a traditional college program that leads to a Bachelor of Science Degree in Business Administration. Faculty responsible for curriculum design and implementation in the same business program was interviewed with the intent of revealing the elements of the program intended to foster students' leadership development.

Kouzes and Posner's (2002) five practices of exemplary leadership, model the way, inspire a shared vision, challenge the process, enable others to act, and encourage the heart, serve as the conceptual framework that is being used to define the leadership behaviors that will be measured. In this study, a traditional college program is a conventional program that consists of eight, 15-week semesters. Each semester is typically comprised of five, three credit hour courses, for a total of between 120 and 124 credit hours required for graduation. Each three credit hour course entails 45 faculty contact hours, with minor variations.

This chapter presents the background and rationale for examining college students' self-reported leadership behaviors with the intent of better understanding their leadership development as it relates to preparation for initial employment in business. This is followed by a statement of the problem, an explanation of the conceptual framework, the primary research question and hypotheses, definitions of terms, and the significance of the study.

Background and Rationale for Describing Leadership Development as a Result of Academic Preparation

While leadership content is present in most business programs, few assess how well they are teaching leadership skills and what students have learned about leadership during the course of their college education. Leadership development has long been central to the mission of business administration programs in higher education (Komives, Lucas, & McMahon, 2007), and more than 60% of the top 50 U.S. business schools publicize that they offer coursework in leadership (Doh, 2003, p. 55). Cavico and Mujtaba (2010) posited, "A fundamental mission of business schools is to help students find employment opportunities, particularly when jobs are scarce in a recessionary economy. Yet there is a larger goal, and that is to produce students who will be business leaders" (p. 107). According to the National Association of Colleges and Employers (2010), or NACE, businesses consider leadership experience among the most important factors, second to only grade point average, when selecting the candidates they hire. In fact, leadership skills were ranked in the top ten most important qualities for candidates (NACE, 2010). Similarly, in the executive summary of a recent Harvard Business School's Global Business Summit, Garvin and Datar (2008) noted that leadership was of primary importance to employers, and admonished that leadership behaviors should be assessed.

The need for confident leaders in business and industry has grown with the increase of competitive pressures (Lang, 2001). Businesses increasingly utilize strategies of continuous improvement and organizational change in response to competition in the highly competitive markets where they operate. This operational style requires leaders "who know how to reorganize existing resources through innovative strategies, make rapid but well-thought-out decisions, and create collaborative work teams to enhance employee productivity" (Morrison, 2003, p. 4). At the same time, "82% of organizations had difficulty finding qualified leaders" (Buss, 2001, p. 46). This shortage of confident, qualified leaders shows no signs of abatement. Colleges and universities that grant degrees in business administration are well-positioned to develop leadership skills in their students because they often offer a series of leadership development activities (Pfeffer, 2009). Yet, as Pfeffer (2009) has noted, there seems to be a "paucity of evaluation of leadership development efforts" (p. 8).

In a recent research paper (Pfeffer, 2009), the author explains that leadership development has long been a mission of higher education. He cites that Harvard Business School's mission "frequently articulated by their former dean, Kim Clark, is to educate leaders who make a difference in the world" (p. 3). Such assertions of leadership development appear in the public documents of most business schools. Moreover, leadership development is a common tenet of higher education in general. Pfeffer (2009) explains that leadership is taken seriously by many companies as well, and cites the considerable sums of money and effort devoted to the development of leaders that can shepherd their firms successfully into the future. Despite the many compelling reasons to develop leaders, higher education has most often failed to answer the call. Pfeffer (2009) posits that at the core of this problem is a lack of assessment. The assumption that the students of business schools acquire the knowledge and self-efficacy required to assume positions of leadership is based on faith rather than data. While businesses regularly utilize assessment centers to "turn learning into practice in realistic situations" (p. 5), such methods are rarely used in business schools. Pfeffer (2009) concludes that assessment is one of the most important areas that business schools need to change if they are serious about leadership development.

There is a body of research that has addressed student leadership development in traditional programs. Some recent examples of research in traditional programs include a 2005 study by Judge where the researcher documented the evolution of an outdoor leadership challenge course used as part of an executive M.B.A. program at the University of Tennessee. The participants in this program took part in an outdoor-based experiential leadership training event designed to be "a potentially transformative capstone personal growth experience that focuses on Kouzes and Posner's (2002) leadership practices inventory" (Judge, 2005, p. 284). Faculty members administer the student version of the Leadership Practices Inventory before and after the course. The resulting feedback enabled Judge to refine the program, achieving incrementally increasing growth in S-LPI scores with each subsequent section of the course (p. 300).

In another example, Barry Z Posner (2009) looked at the LPI scores of seniors at a private university on the west coast. The study compared 384 seniors who had completed a leadership development program as part of the business curriculum for freshmen with 294 seniors enrolled in non-business programs who had not participated in the leadership program. The Student-LPI was used to measure the leadership behaviors of students in both groups. The findings indicated that those who completed the leadership program as freshman scored significantly higher on the S-LPI than the students that did not participate in the leadership program as freshman (p. 560).

Kenary (2010) explored the relationship between service learning experiences and students' self perceptions of their leadership development. The study was conducted using 25 students enrolled in a leadership course for one semester. The participants were divided into 5 groups of five students per work group. These groups worked together for the entire semester. The students completed the S-LPI, along with a 2 question survey designed by the researcher, before and immediately after a service learning experience. At the conclusion of the course and after completing the surveys, the students participated in a focus group moderated by the researcher. The findings indicated statistically significant increases in the students' self perception of their leadership development in four of the five leadership practices described by Kouzes and Posner (2002). The lone exception was the practice called Modeling the Way (Kouzes & Posner, 2002.), which did not change significantly. Based on these findings, the researcher recommended that service learning be incorporated into future leadership courses as a means of developing students' leadership skills.

In sum, leadership development evaluation has been conducted in traditional business programs. The studies by Judge (2005) and Posner (2009) were used to inform practice at their respective institutions. Business administration leadership development programs can affect positive changes in students' self-reported skill and confidence. This study seeks to extend prior research with the intent of informing practice and better preparing students for initial employment.

Statement of the Problem

The need for competent leaders in business and industry has grown with the increase of competitive pressures and the continuing trend toward globalization (Lang, 2001). At the same time, many studies, such as those described in chapter two, have determined that the development of students' leadership abilities is a desirable outcome of a business education. One of the primary purposes of a business program is leadership preparation. The students' readiness to demonstrate a fundamental level of ability as leaders is an important aspect of career preparation for business students. The businesses that will employ them will look to hire those that have learned enough leadership content to feel ready for initial employment.

Some previous research (Komives, Lucas, & McMahon, 2007) indicated that leadership development has long been a mission in higher education. It would follow that the processes used to teach leadership should be identified, and the outcomes correlated. One of the primary purposes of a business program is career preparation. Students' self-reports of their leadership practices as described by Kouzes and Posner (2002) provide a lens for examining the students' perceptions of their ability to apply leadership content. The students' ability to demonstrate a fundamental level of ability as leaders is an important aspect of career preparation for business students. The businesses that will employ them will look to hire those that satisfy their requirements.

Pfeffer (2009) observed that although there are many reasons why leadership development is important, in higher education assessment of leadership is rare. Moreover, he stated that in general, colleges and universities have failed to supply business and industry with adequately prepared leaders. He maintains that the core of the problem is a lack of assessment.

The intent of this study is to determine what elements of a four-year business program help first time job seekers meet employers' expectations for leadership abilities by examining the self-reported leadership behaviors and answers to questions about academic preparation of students at a four-year college in a northeastern state. The curriculum designers of the college have embedded leadership content in various courses. Faculty interviews will attempt to provide insight how instructors often pair the lessons in leadership theory with application exercises, usually in the form of simulations such as case studies. Interviews will also attempt to reveal any additional opportunities to apply leadership content exist outside of the classroom in activities such as student government and case study competition teams. Faculty will be asked to provide accounts of how students may also gain leadership application experience while serving the internships required for graduation. While there is clearly opportunity for leadership development during the course of the business student's education at the college, there has been no documented observations revealing how much these students know about leadership, or which specific courses or activities contributed most to their leadership development.

There is evidence in the literature (Komives, Lucas, & McMahon, 2007, Cavico & Mujtaba ,2010; NACE, 2010; Garvin and Datar, 2008) that suggests that employers expect that business school graduates that they consider for employment possess at least foundational leadership content knowledge combined with some application experience. The college in this study and probably many others as well, has no method currently in place to determine which courses or activities are most effective in fostering students' leadership development, and no systematic method to measure the students' self-perceptions of their leadership skills.

Without obtaining data on the outcomes of teaching leadership, there is no way to be sure that business programs are serving the needs of students and the businesses that will employ them. By administering the S-LPI, which serves as an example of an application of leadership content, to seniors in the business program, it will be possible to determine students' perceptions of their leadership development. Additionally, this study seeks to reveal through student interviews what elements of the management program are perceived by students to teach leadership content, and students' perceptions of what elements provide opportunities for application of the content. By conducting faculty interviews this study will also gather faculty perceptions of the curricular elements intended to teach leadership, and provide insights into what leadership content these seniors know. This study's findings can serve as a guide to future program refinements, with the goal of increasing students' leadership knowledge and application abilities.

Conceptual Framework

The conceptual framework that will guide this study is derived from Kouzes and Posner's (2002) five practices of exemplary leadership. For nearly three decades, Kouzes and Posner (2002) have compiled findings from their research on the dynamic process of leadership. Through case analyses and survey questionnaires, they uncovered five practices of exemplary Leadership that were "common to personal-best leadership experiences" (p. 13). These practices are (a) Model the Way, (b) Inspire a Shared Vision, (c) Challenge the Process, (d) Enable Others to Act, and (e) Encourage the Heart.

Kouzes and Posner (2002) posited "leadership is not at all about personality; it's about practice" (p. 13). The authors affirmed, "Leadership is an identifiable set of skills and abilities that are available to all of us" (2002, p. 23). If one of the missions of higher education is to prepare students for careers, then business administration programs should be concerned with the development of students' leadership skills and abilities, since employers seek to hire individuals that posses these skills and abilities and can actively lead others. The five practices of exemplary leadership that comprise the core of this study's conceptual framework follow.

Model the Way

The practice of modeling the way requires leaders to first find their voice, and then set the example.

Find your voice. Kouzes and Posner (2002) admonished that "to effectively model the behavior they expect of others, leaders must first be clear about their guiding principles" (p. 14). This clarity is a prerequisite to what the authors refer to as "finding your voice" (p. 43). An important part of students' preparation for careers in business is the development of leadership competencies. To become effective leaders, students must learn whom they are both intellectually and morally, and effectively communicate from that orientation. By speaking and acting from the heart consistently to demonstrate their commitment, leaders build commitment from their followers.

Set the example. Effective leaders align their actions first with their own values, and then they must align their actions with the shared values of the organization. Kouzes and Posner (2002) recalled, "The personal-best projects we heard about in our research were all distinguished by relentless effort, steadfastness, competence, and attention to detail" (p. 14). Modeling the way involves earning and maintaining the respect of followers. People are drawn to and subsequently follow other people first, they become attracted to the plan later.

Inspire a Shared Vision

To engage in the practice of inspiring a shared vision, leaders must envision the future and then enlist others.

Envision the future. Leaders' ability to envision the future sets them apart from others. Leaders inspire others by effectively communicating their vision for the future. Kouzes and Posner (2002) stated "To enlist people in a vision, leaders must know their constituents and speak their language. People must believe that leaders understand their words and have their interests at heart" (p. 16).

Enlist others. Effective leaders convince followers that their vision for the future will be good for everyone in the organization. The key to convincing others is enthusiasm and consistency. A leader that enthusiastically speaks with a consistent message from the heart is difficult to resist. To become effective leaders, students must learn to inspire others by sharing their passion. Enthusiasm spreads, igniting the flame of inspiration, if it is genuine. Attempts to inspire others that are less than genuine, or not from the heart, will often be sensed by followers, and typically fall short of their intended goals.

Challenge the Process

The practice of challenging the process consists of searching for opportunities and experimenting and taking risks.

Search for opportunities. Leaders are agents of change, described by Kouzes and Posner (2002) as pioneers (p. 17). Every leadership challenge involves change. Without change, there would be a very limited role for leaders. Opportunities for improvement rise from throughout the organization, and leaders must be able to recognize and adopt these ideas when constituents present them. The authors posited, "It might be more accurate, then, to say that leaders are *early adopters* of innovation" (p. 17).

Experiment and take risks. Change involves the risk of failure, but effective leaders proceed anyway. These pioneers recognize that these challenges are opportunities to improve. Effective leaders have learned to view change as a leadership opportunity, and with it comes the possibility of both organizational and personal growth. Kouzes and Posner (2002) caution that repeated failures will not make a good leader. Rather, learning from failures can make leaders more effective in future efforts. The authors quoted Warren Bennis who wrote, "Leaders learn by leading, and they learn best by leading in the face of obstacles" (p. 17). Obstacles shape the learning and specific characteristics of developing leaders.

Graduating business students often seek positions in business that include a leadership component. If higher education has adequately prepared them, they will be able to recognize and act upon leadership opportunities as they arise, in the process advancing their careers. These opportunities to challenge the process and assume leadership roles can transform organizations for the better, provided the leaders have developed the necessary skills. Without this leadership development, they are likely to follow others that were ready to accept the challenge. For these followers, career advancement will proceed more slowly, if at all.

Enable Others To Act

The practice of enabling others to act is comprised of two elements, fostering collaboration and strengthening others.

Foster collaboration. According to Kouzes and Posner (2002), exemplary leaders "foster collaboration and build trust and make it possible for others to do good work" (p. 18). Creating a climate of trust is critical to organizational success. Without trust in their team members, leaders try to do everything themselves, or micro-manage the efforts of others. The lack of trust in followers by leaders usually results in followers not trusting the leader. Such a climate wastes the potential of the team's members. Students will need to have developed leadership skills and be confident in their abilities if they are to effectively nurture collaborative work teams.

Strengthen others. They share power and responsibility with others, and in the process, they motivate their constituents while benefitting from their inputs. Constituent motivation involves intrinsic work attributes such as authority, autonomy, recognition, and achievement. Through this process, constituents also become leaders that are likely to direct their energies for the good of the organization.

Encourage the Heart

For leaders to effectively practice encouraging the heart, they must recognize contributions and celebrate values and victories.

Recognize contributions. The process of continual improvement is, by definition, endless. Constituents can become demoralized and exhausted without frequent encouragement. Kouzes and Posner stated, "Genuine acts of caring uplift the spirits and draw people forward. Encouragement can come from dramatic gestures or simple actions" (p. 19). Without recognition, associates are unlikely to expend the extra effort required of extraordinary contributions.

Celebrate the values and victories. Leaders are responsible for showing appreciation and celebrating successes, large and small. The methods of recognition are widely varied, but to be effective constituents must perceive them as genuine. If the encouragement is not perceived to be genuine, constituents will turn away and the credibility of the leader will be comprised. Credibility, once damaged, can be difficult or impossible to regain. If done properly, however, celebrations and rituals become part of the organization's culture that can be an enduring source of inspiration. Students will need to be firmly grounded in their values and the shared values of the organization if there are to be perceived as genuine by the associates they lead.

All of the leadership practices combine to form an effective model of leadership. Students do not have innate knowledge of these practices, they must learn them. Learning in the field after graduation is haphazard at best. Higher education is best positioned to supply the leadership training that students can then apply throughout their careers.

Table 1

Conceptual Framework: Kouzes and Posner's Leadership Practices Theory

Leadership Behavior	Description
1. Challenge the Process	Leading involves change. Change requires altering existing processes. Leaders must be willing to take risks when challenging the status quo

2. Inspire a Shared Vision

Ability to persuade others that the leader's goals and visions for the future are the same as theirs.

3. Enable Others to Act

Effective leaders cultivate collaboration and trust. Leaders and followers are trusted and supported in their efforts.

4. Model the Way

Leader sets the example of required behavior within the organization. Also helps define climate and culture of the organization by providing an example

5. Encourage the Heart

Leader uses intrinsic rewards to motivate individuals within the organization. Recognition, achievement, advancement, growth, and increased responsibility are among the tools leaders use to make members of the organization feel valued and spur them on to greater achievements.

Research Questions

The following research questions will guide this study. The first question, it's five related sub-questions, and questions two through four address final-year business students in the School of Management at a small college in a northeastern state. Research questions five through seven are directed to full-time faculty in the School of Management at that same college.

Research question 1. What are business students' self-reports of their leadership behaviors as articulated by Kouzes and Posner and measured by the S-LPI (Kouzes & Posner, 2002).

Research question 1.a. What are business students' self-reports of the leadership behavior Model the Way.

Research question 1.b. What are business students' self-reports of the leadership behavior Inspire a Shared Vision.

Research question 1.c. What are the business students' self-reports of the leadership behavior Challenge the Process.

Research question 1.d. What are business students' self-reports of the leadership behavior Enable Others to Act.

Research question 1.e. What are business students' self-reports of the leadership behavior Encourage the Heart.

Research question 2. What are business students' self-reports of their preparedness to meet potential employers' expectations of a candidate's leadership development?

Research question 3. What are business students' perceptions of the elements of the curriculum that contributed most to their leadership development?

Research question 4. What are business students' perceptions of other elements of the college experience that may prepare them for leadership?

Research question 5. How does the management curriculum, as reported by program faculty, help students acquire leadership content knowledge?

Research question 6. How does the management curriculum, as reported by program faculty, provide students with experiences to apply leadership content knowledge?

Research question 7. Are there any other elements of the college experience that may prepare students for leadership?

Definition of Terms

Table 2 contains conceptual definitions of key terms, as applied in this study.

Table 2

Definitions of Terms

Elements of the College Experience	Leadership content knowledge and application simulations as designed in curriculum
Four year college	An accredited institution offering a course of study leading to a Bachelor of Science in Business Administration degree.

Leadership

"Inducing followers to act for certain goals that represent the values and the motivations—the wants and needs, the aspirations and expectations—of both leaders and followers" (Burns, 1978, p. 381)

Leadership Behaviors

Challenge the Process: Leading involves change. Change requires altering existing processes. Leaders must be willing to take risks when challenging the status quo.

Inspire a Shared Vision: Ability to persuade others that the leader's goals and visions for the future are the same as theirs.

Enable Others to Act: Effective leaders cultivate collaboration and trust. Leaders and followers are trusted and supported in their efforts.

Model the Way: Leader sets the example of required behavior within the organization. Also helps define climate and culture of the organization by providing an example

Encourage the Heart: Leader uses intrinsic rewards to motivate individuals within the organization. Recognition, achievement, advancement, growth, and increased responsibility are among the tools leaders use to make members of the organization feel valued and spur them on to greater achievements.

Leadership Content Knowledge
Subject information within the curriculum specifically focusing on leadership

Management Curriculum
Curriculum of all courses leading to a 4 year degree from the School of Management

Program Faculty
All full-time faculty in the School of Management.

Traditional format
A college program of study comprised of 15 week semesters, with 45 faculty

contact hours per 3 credit-hour course.

Significance of the Study

The intent of this study is to determine what elements of a four-year business program help first time job seekers meet employers' expectations for leadership abilities. This by examining the self-reported leadership behaviors of students and interviews with faculty responsible for the design and implementation of elements of the curriculum intended to foster leadership development at a four-year college in a northeastern state. More specifically, the *Student Leadership Practices Inventory* (Kouzes & Posner, 2002), or S-LPI, combined with interview questions will be administered to students enrolled in the final year of a traditional college program that leads to a Bachelor of Science degree in Business Administration.

Additionally, the researcher will interview program faculty with the intent of revealing how they go about developing students' leadership abilities.

The study is significant for three reasons. First, the self assessment business students will provide a lens to compare their reported leadership development with the reports of other groups that have previously taken the S-LPI. This may prove valuable not only to the college in this study, but to other business programs with similar curriculum design.

Second, this study will provide information of direct value to the faculty of the participating program. Outcomes may influence the possible introduction of a leadership course or module, or other changes in curriculum, as has been suggested in other studies (Judge, 2005; Kenary, 2010; Posner, 2009).

Third, this study will seek to add to the leadership education knowledge base. Since no previous studies have assessed the leadership development of business students at this college, or provided a view of the intended and enacted curriculum along with students' accounts of their academic preparation for leadership, this study has the potential to provide important baseline information.

Chapter 2: Review of the Related Literature

This chapter presents a review of literature related to trends in leadership likely to impact undergraduate business students, elements of various business curricula designed to teach leadership, and a review of some of the available instruments that can provide a lens through which the researcher can examine and quantify undergraduate business students' leadership development.

Leadership Trends

According to Porter (2008), effective leadership is required if an organization is to create maximum value. Moreover, value creation is an act of leadership (p. xxvi). Value creation is then fundamental purpose of business, and successfully creating value is dependent upon the effectiveness of its leaders. Given the importance of effective leadership in business, institutions of higher education must recognize the importance of leadership development as part of students' career preparation.

Another trend that supports the need for teaching leadership in undergraduate business programs is the increasing use of personality assessments in the workplace. According to Birkman International (2007), personality assessments were used by 65% of companies in 2006. One of the key areas most often assessed is that of leadership development. These assessments are used both for pre-employment screening and as an instrument to inform promotion and succession planning. One of the most popular is the Predictive Index, which has been in use since 1955. Koski and Tubbs (2010) wrote "one of the most vexing problems for any organization is the ability to accurately and efficiently assess the leadership potential of both new hires and existing talent within the organization" (p. 74.). The Predictive index has proven to be reliable and valid (p. 74.), and is in use in over 125 countries, in over 58 different languages.

The Predictive Index, combined with the many other leadership assessment instruments, serve as a gatekeeper in the path of business graduates career advancement. Given the prevalence of these instruments, and businesses reliance upon them, career preparation should include curriculum designed to develop the attributes measured. Since one of the primary attributes measured is leadership, it follows that undergraduate business programs should have some emphasis on leadership development.

Drew (2006, p. 117) wrote that the academic environment is becoming more like businesses, signaling an emerging trend in academe. He posited that academic leaders and their organizations could benefit from the utilization of a 360 leadership assessment. The implication for this paper is that even business students that intend to seek careers in academe rather than business will likely face some assessment of their leadership development during their careers.

The AACSB has operationalized the inclusion of leadership studies in the curricula of business programs. They maintain that "undergraduate degree programs in business educate students in a broad range of knowledge and skills as a basis for careers in business" (p. 57). Students then would need to have achieved a level of proficiency in their leadership development that would satisfy the requirements of the businesses that would hire them.

Leadership Curriculum in Undergraduate Business Programs

Practically every undergraduate business program today addresses the topic of leadership in its curriculum. Leadership content first entered business schools' curriculum at the MBA level in the 1990's (Polito, Berry, & Watson, n.d.) in response to charges that business schools were producing individuals with analytic and decision making skills, but were lacking leadership abilities. Additional pressure resulted when, as cited by Polito, Berry, and Watson, the AACSB concluded in a 1990 study that business schools were not preparing students for leadership (Polito et al, p. 2). Business schools acted quickly, and by the mid 1990's 20% of offerings in executive education focused on leadership. The strategies for incorporating leadership into the curriculum varied widely, but nonetheless, instruction in leadership spread to undergraduate business programs as well.

Often embedded in various courses, programs routinely offer instruction in leadership theory, tracing the various developments from the early trait theorists to the contemporary, behavior based models. Leadership studies are frequently linked to ethics, often under the heading of ethical leadership. While instruction in leadership content is ubiquitous across business curricula, the approaches to exposing students to applications of leadership content vary widely. They run the gamut from reading textbook accounts of the behavior of leaders, to simulation exercises such as case studies, to first-hand experience leading in the world of business with mentors.

Taylor (2007) recounted an example of the mentoring approach taking place at the Fogelman College of Business and Economics at the University of Memphis. The author teamed with Austin Baker, a local entrepreneur, to form MILE: The Memphis Institute for Leadership Education. This mentoring program pairs top undergraduate business students with leaders from the Memphis business community. The students experience business leadership with business professionals, and are afforded the opportunity to network with other program mentors. Among the experiences available to the students, are job shadowing, attending professional meetings, and mock interviewing. The Mentors benefit from the opportunity to screen and recruit the business schools top students.

Godson (2007) described another approach to teaching leadership. She wrote, "Advance Collegiate Schools of Business cites faculty apathy as being the greatest single impediment to increasing the emphasis on ethical education in the business curriculum" (2007, p. 48). To this charge, she replied that teaching ethical leadership must extend beyond the classroom. At Baylor University, they have created an Ethical Leadership Case Competition, where students' solutions to various problems are presented before qualified judges. The author emphasized that business schools play an important role in helping future leaders prepare to be effective, ethical leaders. Exposing students to ethical models designed to simulate situations that they would encounter as leaders can increase their "ethical I. Q." The author noted the AACSB requires that ethics be taught in some form to qualify for accreditation, but it does not specify how it should be done. Anne Grinols, the Assistant Dean at Baylor Business feels that case studies, and specifically a case study competition, are the most effective method of teaching ethical leadership. The author concurs, and lauds the efforts at Baylor.

According to a report from Hood College (1988), the business curriculum at Hood addresses leadership and ethics jointly through a combination of traditional coursework and community service. In their core courses, students receive ethical dilemmas embedded in the curriculum, designed to provide an understanding of leadership ethics. In their later courses, they "develop a tolerance for ambiguity and for the absence of clear solutions in the world they will enter" (p. 16). They then render service in the Greater Washington area, alongside faculty and staff, gaining leadership experience in the process.

Hunt and Weintraub (2004) described a business program in which MBA students are trained to serve as coaches to undergraduate business students as part of an advanced elective on leadership. These MBA students have no power to evaluate or punish the undergraduate students in any way, rather they exercise their expert leadership through their ability to help with writing and other assignments. The undergraduate students at the college are required to participate in the program at two separate times during their college careers. For the undergraduates the goal is to "develop greater self-awareness in exercising the behavior skills of leadership" (p. 39). The coaches receive 8 hours of training in developmental coaching in areas such as how to build a coaching friendly relationship, observing effectively, helping the learner to define goals for participation in the program, listening, and providing useful feedback (p. 39). In this program both the MBA students and the undergraduates have the opportunity to learn about and develop important leadership behaviors.

Some business programs utilize a modular approach to teaching leadership. These can range from 1 day seminars to multiple week immersions in leadership. A two week example of this was developed by Judge (2005), who documented the evolution of an outdoor leadership challenge course utilized as part of an executive M.B.A. program at the University of Tennessee (2005). The participants of this program took part in an outdoor-based experiential leadership training event designed to be "a potentially transformative capstone personal growth experience that focuses on Kouzes and Posner's leadership practices inventory" (2005, p. 284). Students were put into situations where they had to lead their peers through a variety of different challenges, from a variety of perspectives. Faculty members administer the student version of the Leadership Practices Inventory before and after the course. The resulting feedback has enabled Judge to refine the program, achieving incrementally increasing growth with each subsequent section of the course (p. 300). Many key elements of this course have are now incorporated into the undergraduate program, notably as part of the Ignite programs three day retreat.

Murdoch and Brammer (2011) recently described a leadership development program for physicians that utilize an instrument developed by the National Center for Healthcare Leadership. The Health Leadership Competency Model relies on physician self assessment in 26 areas under three domains: executive, transformation, and people. Physicians rank themselves from 1 (low) to 5 (high) in each area before and after the training program. The table below (p. 53) lists the areas assessed and the pre and post program self-reported rankings.

Table 3

Health Leadership Competency

Competency	Entry Ranking Average	Exit Ranking Average
Achievement Orientation	3.4	4.1
Analytical Thinking	2.7	4.0
Community Orientation	2.9	4.1
Financial Skills	3.3	4.0
Information Seeking	3.0	3.8
Innovative Thinking	3.2	4.2
Strategic Orientation	3.1	4.2
Accountability	3.1	4.2
Change Leadership	2.8	4.2
Collaboration	2.7	3.7
Communication Skills	2.5	3.3
Impact and Influence	2.9	3.7
Initiative	3.3	3.9
Information Technology	3.1	3.8
Organizational Awareness	3.0	3.7
Performance Measurement	3.4	4.3
Process Management	3.1	4.0
Project Management	3.0	4.0
Human Resource Mgmt.	2.8	3.9

Interpersonal Understanding	3.0	4.1
Professionalism	3.3	4.2
Relationship Building	3.1	4.1
Self-Confidence	3.1	4.1
Self-Development	2.7	3.5
Talent Development	2.8	4.1
Team Leadership	2.8	4.1

The instrument was the only assessment used to determine the effectiveness of the physician leadership program, which operated for 5 years and was deemed a success. The authors posited that the program's success could be attributed to "exposure to new learning by diverse health care experts and thought leaders, and increased awareness of topics and actions relevant to effective medical leadership and management" (p. 55). Also credited with positively influencing program outcomes were "review of articles, books and other materials that increased knowledge and understanding of key issues and topics important in health care leadership" (p. 55) along with the benefits of group dynamics within the cohort of learners.

Harvard Business School emphasizes leadership studies in its undergraduate business program. In one portion of its business program the school offers a one week *Summer Venture in Management program* to seniors (2008). In this program, HBS faculty utilizes a case study method of instruction, and emphasizes, "The impact they can have on their community and the world through business leadership. HBS case studies are widely used as a method of simulation by business programs throughout higher education, in addition to forming the backbone of leadership instruction at Harvard.

Heames and Service (2003) proposed, based on their leadership research, that by moving from the "old control model of teaching, managing, and leading based on stability and power to a new enterprise model based on speed and constant self-innovation"(p. 118). By shifting the way business courses are taught from the traditional teacher-centered classroom to a student-centered one, students learn to lead their own problem-based learning. The authors suggest that classroom practices can become the foundations of effective business leadership after graduation, and suggest six instructional techniques as a starting point for those willing to redesign their approach to teaching.

The title of the first technique or guideline is *Class Objectives.* The authors direct the teacher to list the lessons learning objectives on the board, and have the students lead their own discussion exploring the objectives. By taking part in the process that includes an initial discussion, defining terms, exploring connections, and giving examples, the "students clarified their understandings, which made them more likely to think as leaders" (p. 120).

The second guideline, *Fit the Students,* admonishes instructors to direct discussions "so that they fit the students' interests, yet are related to class objectives" (p.120). If the objectives are not completely met, then the instructor may present a brief executive summary at the conclusion of the class, thus filling any gaps encountered.

Reflect on relationships was the third guideline discussed in the article. The focus of this guideline is getting students to apply theoretical knowledge to real life situations. Since students may have limited work experience, they may need to look to school activities such as sports, or relationships with friends, parents, or others.

Emphasizing the Unorthodox, the fourth guideline, encourages the instructor to handle each class differently (p. 120) and to explore blending of styles and methods. The authors offer many examples such as having students teach the material to the instructor, using role-play, presentations, and group work to list a few. The authors encourage instructors to experiment with and continually change their methods, reasoning that in the world of business they will encounter a wide assortment of individuals utilizing many different approaches to their work. Consistently changing methods of instruction therefore better prepares students for the dynamic environment of business.

The fifth guideline titled *Expand Opportunities for Critical Assessment* the authors admonish that multiple choice exams should be avoided, since in real life there are few occasions when we can choose from *a, b, c, or d.* The researchers suggest that a take-home exam is a better simulation of a real-world problem solving or fact finding task.

The sixth and final guideline, *Use Technology to Add Value,* stresses that technology should never be used to replace preparation and spontaneous thinking. The authors insist it should add to the richness of the communication, instead of using it as a crutch.

Instruments for Quantifying Leadership Development

In 1985, Bernard Bass introduced the Multifactor Leadership Questionnaire. The instrument at that time was comprised of seven leadership factors. These were charisma, inspirational, intellectual stimulation, individualized consideration, contingent reward, management-by-exception and laisse-faire leadership (Avolio, Bass, & Jung, 1999). In the years between 1985 and 1999, Avolio joined Bass, and the researchers revised the instrument numerous times.

The authors derived the structure for the MLQ from Burn's description of transforming leadership (Burns, 1978). According to the authors description of the initial testing of the instrument, "Seventy-eight executives were asked to describe a leader who had influenced what was important to them in their roles as leaders, and how they thought the best leaders were able to get others to go beyond their own self-interests for the good of the group" (Avolio et al., 1999, p. 443). These executives were initially evaluated on a list of 142 factors. The researchers separated these factors into two groups, transformational and transactional contingent reward leadership. Eleven judges reviewed the factors, with eighty percent or greater agreement on each factor required for future inclusion. The final version of the original MLQ was comprised of 73 factors grouped under six broader factor headings. Those six headings are charisma, intellectual stimulation, individualized consideration, contingent reward, active management by exception, and passive avoidant leadership. The researchers administered the instrument to 176 US Army colonels instructed to describe their superiors. The six-factor model proved effective, and after many revisions, the current model utilizes six-factors once again. The United States armed forces still use the MLQ to assess leadership development.

Wide ranges of educational programs assess leadership development. Many of the instruments are qualitative, and specifically designed for the program. An example of this is the assessment piloted at Massachusetts General Hospital and Yale University Health Management Program (Robbins, Bradley, Spicer, & Mecklenburg, 2008).The instrument format is a structured interview with a four point rating scale. Graduate students and early careerist in the healthcare industry seeking senior leadership positions are assessed using a qualitative instrument that measures 52 competencies categorized into four domains. "Early experience with the tool suggests that it can facilitate career planning among graduate *students*, early careerists, and their mentors. Further, the tool can help directors of both academic and practitioner programs identify strengths and gaps in their existing curricula or training programs" (Robbins et al., 2008, p. 188)

By 1987, Kouzes and Posner had compiled four years of research and published *The Leadership Challenge.* Their research on leadership did establish some conformity to the leadership traits theory. They asked more than 75,000 respondents what values and traits they looked for in leaders and found that in a period spanning fifteen years from 1987 to 2002 that the list of traits had remained constant. According to their research, admired leaders should be honest, forward looking, inspiring, and competent. The majority of respondents consistently saw these top four traits as essential characteristics from the initial compilation of data in 1987 until the subsequent compilation in 1995. The top characteristic labeled "honest" was agreed to be important to 83% of those questioned in 1987, a figure that increased to 88% in the 2002 report. The trait entitled forward-looking rose from 62% in 1987 to 71% in 2002. The number three characteristic as ranked by the survey results, competent, decreased 1 percent from 67 percent in 1987 to 66 percent in 2002. The fourth most agreed upon characteristic, inspiring, increased seven percentage points from 58 percent in 1987 to 65 percent in 2002. The order of ranking of these top characteristics changed slightly over this time, with competent rising to the third position in 2002 edging out inspiring by 1 percentage point. The rest of the comprehensive list of characteristics each garnered less than a majority position based on agreement of the respondents, although the characteristics themselves and their respective ranking remained consistent over the time of comparison (Kouzes & Posner, 1995).

From the study we may conclude that effective leaders are thought by others to posses at least the top four characteristics, however it does not necessarily follow that anyone exhibiting these traits will become an effective leader. According to Kouzes & Posner, "Leadership is not at all about personality; it's about practice" (p. 13). Effective leaders can not be consistently manufactured by simply selecting individuals with the traits discussed above and training them, rather it was found that those that became effective leaders did so by following a common path of action. Part of the common path is a focus on a committing style referred to as *transformational leadership.* Describing transformational leadership the authors cite Burns, whom explained that this style "raises the level of human conduct and ethical aspiration of both the leader and the led, and thus it has a transforming effect on both" (2002, p. 153). Kouzes & Posner examined these actions and broke them down into their "Five Practices of Exemplary Leadership". The five practices are as follows: Model the Way, Inspire a Shared Vision, Challenge the Process, Enable Others to Act, and Encourage the Heart. The process is the key, not the traits. Those individual who can successfully execute the process will likely posses the characteristics noted, but not everyone that possesses the characteristics will succeed in executing the process. The top four characteristics, at least, are probably required of an effective leader, but their presence is not an assurance of success.

One of the most important aspects of Kouzes and Posner's work was the development of an assessment instrument, the Leadership Practices Inventory, or LPI. The LPI consists of questions designed to assess the relative strength of the five leadership behaviors. Respondents submit answers in a Likert scale format. The LPI-self is a self-administered assessment; the authors designed the LPI-observer to be completed by others familiar with the behaviors of the subject of the study. The student version, or SLPI, is similar to the LPI-self only designed for students who have yet to lead in the workplace

Wide ranges of educational programs assess leadership development. Many of the instruments are qualitative, and specifically designed for the program. An example of this is the assessment piloted at Massachusetts General Hospital and Yale University Health Management Program (Robbins, Bradley, Spicer, & Mecklenburg, 2008).The instrument format is a structured interview with a four point rating scale. Graduate students and early careerist in the healthcare industry seeking senior leadership positions are assessed using a qualitative instrument that measures 52 competencies categorized into four domains. "Early experience with the tool suggests that it can facilitate career planning among graduate *students*, early careerists, and their mentors. Further, the tool can help directors of both academic and practitioner programs identify strengths and gaps in their existing curricula or training programs" (Robbins et al., 2008, p. 188)

Anderson developed The Leadership Circle Profile or TLCP (2006). According to the author, the instrument is "the first competency-based 360-degree assessment tool to measure behavior at various stages of adult development, to link patterns of action with habits of thought" (p. 175), and organizes information into a display that draws attention to the most critical information.

The instrument is visually depicted as a circle, with the top half of the circle, labeled "creative" is divided into 18 creative competencies. The bottom half of the circle is labeled "reactive". The author asserts that these two orientations result in different outcomes, with the creative orientation leading to intended results and the reactive orientation leading the maintaining the current situation. Anderson cites research by Kegan (1994) which concludes that 70 percent of adults are working from a reactive orientation, and that only 10 percent ever evolve beyond the creative orientation.

The circle is also divided left and right, with the left labeled as "relationship" and the right labeled "task". These categories reflect the theories of numerous leadership researchers (Stogill, 1948; Likert, 1967; Blake and Mouton, 1978). When combined with the corresponding creative or reactive orientation, the user of the instrument is provided with a depiction of the leader's current competencies, along with a suggested path for improvement.

Reed, Vidaver-Cohen, and Colwell (2011) recently developed an instrument to measure executive servant leadership. The focus of the article is ethical leadership and the leadership concepts that share dimensions of ethical leadership. According to the authors these concepts are transformational, authentic, spiritual, and servant leadership. The instrument developed by the researchers, the Executive Servant Leadership Scale or ESLS, is described in the article along with a discussion of its contributions and limitations.

The authors choose servant leadership from the four concepts because "servant leaders are those who manage organizational challenges by subordinating personal interests to those of organizational stakeholders" (p. 2.). All of the ethical concepts are characterized by concern for others and integrity, but only the servant leader acts as a moral manager for the organization. The servant leader develops others through modeling attractive behaviors, thus creating new servant leaders.

The researchers indentified 55 items to measure key dimensions of servant leadership as expressed by the behaviors of top executives. Participants rated these items on a 4 point Likert scale (strongly disagree – strongly agree).

The key dimension items were grouped into five first-order factors. The factors are; interpersonal support, building community, altruism, egalitarianism, and moral integrity. Interpersonal support helps organizational members develop their potential while shaping the organizational culture into one that encourages growth and service. Building community, both inside and outside of the organization, involves valuing individual differences, encouraging cooperation, and inspiring commitment. All stakeholders are considered, with specific attention given to improving the communities in which they operate. Altruism is defined by the authors as "unselfish concern for others manifested in constructive service" (p. 11). On the ESLS the top executive altruism "is operationalized by serving others willingly with no expectation of reward, sacrificing personal benefit to meet employee needs" (p. 11). Egalitarianism is defined by the authors as "rejecting the notion that leaders are inherently superior to other organizational members" (p.11). Egalitarian executives welcome constructive criticism, learning from their employees and inviting input from all levels. Moral integrity involves promoting transparency and honesty throughout the organization. Table 4 shows the ESLS questionnaire.

Table 4

ESLS Questionnaire

My Organization's Top Executive...

(1) Invests time and energy developing others' potential

(2) Considers the effects of organizational decisions on the
    Community

(3) Effectively thinks through complex problems

(4) Maintains high ethical standards

(5) Inspires others to lead through service

(6) Recognizes when employee morale is low without
   Asking

(7) Looks for ways to make others successful

(8) Encourages open exchange of information throughout
   the organization

(9) Sacrifices personal benefit to meet employee needs

(10) Encourages debate of his/her ideas

(11) Serves others willingly with no expectation of reward

(12) Inspires employee trust

(13) Invites constructive criticism

(14) Shares power with others throughout the
   Organization

(15) Nurtures employee leadership potential

(16) Encourages employees to volunteer in the
   Community

(17) Seems able to tell if something is going wrong in the

Organization

(18) Refuses to use manipulation or deceit to achieve
his/her goals

(19) Promotes empathy and tolerance throughout the
Organization

(20) Encourages a spirit of cooperation among employees

(21) Inspires organizational commitment

(22) Places the interests of others before self-interest

(23) Expresses genuine enjoyment in serving others

(24) Willingly shares credit for organizational
Accomplishments

(25) Treats all employees with dignity and respect

(26) Demonstrates clear understanding of how to attain
organizational goals

(27) Displays interest in learning from employees,
regardless of their level in the organization

(28) Tries to build consensus among employees on important decisions

(29) Ensures greatest decision-making control given to employees most affected by decision

(30) Solves organizational problems with new and creative ideas

(31) Refuses to compromise ethical principles in order to Achieve success

(32) Freely admits his/her mistakes

(33) Promotes transparency and honesty throughout the Organization

(34) Takes time to talk to employees on a personal level

(35) Follows through on what he/she promises to do

(36) Articulates a clear direction for the organization's Future

(37) Listens carefully to others

(38) Looks for new ways to make employees' jobs easier

(39) Believes our organization should give back to the
Community

(40) Values integrity more than profit or personal gain

(41) Believes employees should be given freedom to
handle difficult situations in the way they feel is best

(42) Prefers serving others to being served by others

(43) Demonstrates sensitivity to employees' personal
obligations outside the workplace

(44) Enthusiastically celebrates others' accomplishments

(45) Believes our organization has a duty to improve the
community in which it operates

(46) Values diversity and individual differences in the
Organization

(47) Consistently tries to bring out the best in others

(48) Believes employees should be provided with work
    experiences that enable them to develop new skills

(49) Demonstrates concern for employees' personal
    well-being

(50) Engages in community service and volunteer
    activities outside of work

(51) Makes employee career development an organizational
    Priority

(52) Welcomes ideas and input from employees at all
    levels of the organization

(53) Creates a feeling of belonging in our organization

(54) Communicates candidly with others

(55) Models the behavior he/she expects from others in
    the organization

    The authors concluded by acknowledging that while the concept of servant leadership is not new, instruments designed to measure the construct have appeared only in the last ten years. During the past decade, scandals have occurred in business, sports, government, and other organizations, giving rise to a heightened level of concern about ethical leadership. They offer the ESLS as a starting point in the assessment of our executive leaders.

Summary of the Chapter

There is a trend toward employers being increasingly concerned with the development of leadership abilities in candidates for employment. The use of screening instruments increasingly influences decisions related to employment and promotion in a wide range of organizations.

Leadership content knowledge is present in nearly all business programs, often embedded in various courses and the texts that accompany them. Methods of delivering application opportunities vary widely. They run the gamut from reading textbook accounts of the behavior of leaders, to simulation exercises such as case studies, to first-hand experience leading in the world of business with mentors.

Instruments for assessing leadership development include the Multifactor Leadership Questionnaire (Bass, 1985) and the Leadership Practices Inventory (Kouzes and Posner, 1987). Numerous other instruments have been introduced since, most based, at least in part on these early models. Many are designed for specific applications, such as physicians who manage operations at health care facilities, or to measure ethical behaviors of top executives. The SLPI (Kouzes and Posner, 1995) remains the most widely utilized instrument for student self assessment.

Chapter 3: Research Methodology And Design

Introduction to the Chapter

This chapter describes the research design and methodology for this single case study. The purpose of the study was to describe how students and faculty in the participating school of management perceive the program develops the students' leadership skills. This study proceeded in two complementary ways. The researcher examined students' perceptions of their leadership behaviors along with faculty accounts of the program elements pertaining to leadership. In the first, Kouzes and Posner's (2002) student version of the Leadership Practices Inventory or S-LPI was administered to students in their final year of the business program leading to a Bachelor of Science degree. The self-reported accounts of leadership development by students provided baseline information about the extent of their leadership content knowledge as defined by the study's conceptual framework. Student responses to additional questions were gathered to elicit their accounts of where during their education they learned about leadership and where during their education they had the opportunity to apply this content knowledge. Faculty interviews focused on the elements of the curriculum and overall college experience intended to foster students' leadership development. The study was conducted at a private, four-year college in a northeastern state.

This chapter is organized into the following sections: the restatement of the problem, research questions, definitions of terms, design of study, population and sample, protection of human subjects, data-collection activities, data-analysis procedures, and limitations of the study.

Restatement of the Problem

The need for competent leaders in business and industry has grown with the increase of competitive pressures and the continuing trend toward globalization (Lang, 2001). At the same time, many studies, such as those described in chapter two, have determined that the development of students' leadership abilities is a desirable outcome of a business education. One of the primary purposes of a business program is leadership preparation. The students' readiness to demonstrate a fundamental level of ability as leaders is an important aspect of career preparation for business students. The businesses that will employ them will look to hire those that have learned enough leadership content to feel ready for initial employment.

Buss (2001) wrote, "82% of organizations had difficulty finding qualified leaders" (p. 46). This shortage of confident, qualified leaders shows no signs of abatement. According to Pfeffer (2009), colleges and universities that grant degrees in business administration are well-positioned to develop leadership skills in their students because they often offer a series of leadership development activities. Yet, as Pfeffer (2009) has noted, there seems to be a "paucity of evaluation of leadership development efforts" (p. 8). A review of the literature reveals that there are only infrequent attempts by non AACSB (Association to Advance Collegiate Schools of Business) schools to correlate the elements of curriculum intended to teach about leadership with the perceptions of students regarding their readiness to be leaders upon graduation.

Students' self-reports of their leadership practices as described by Kouzes and Posner (2002) provide a lens for examining the students' perceptions of their ability to apply leadership content. The S-LPI survey has been administered to thousands of individuals with a proven record of reliability and validity. The Kouzes and Posner (2002) model is based on five sets of leadership behaviors:

Model the Way, Inspire a Shared Vision, Challenge the Process, Enable Others to Act, and Encourage the Heart. The wide spread acceptance of the model combined with the proven reliability and validity of the LPI prompted the researcher to adopt this as a conceptual framework.

In sum, the purpose of study is to describe how students and faculty perceive the program develops the students' leadership skills. Additionally, this study will allow for comparison between the perceptions of students and faculty, with any discrepancies providing the opportunity for future research.

Research Questions

The following research questions will guide this study.

Research question 1. What are business students' self-reports about their leadership behaviors as articulated by Kouzes and Posner and measured by the S-LPI (Kouzes & Posner, 2002).

Research question 1a. What are business students' self-reports about the leadership behavior Model the Way.

Research question 1b. What are business students' self-reports about the leadership behavior Inspire a Shared Vision.

Research question 1c. What are the business students' self-reports about the leadership behavior Challenge the Process.

Research question 1d. What are business students' self-reports about the leadership behavior Enable Others to Act.

Research question 1e. What are business students' self-reports about the leadership behavior Encourage the Heart.

Research question 2. What are business students' self-reports about their preparedness to meet potential employers' expectations of a candidate's leadership development?

Research question 3. What are business students' perceptions about the elements of the curriculum that contributed most to their leadership development?

Research question 4. What are business students' perceptions about other elements of the college experience that may prepare them for leadership?

Research question 5. How does the management curriculum, as reported by program faculty, help students acquire leadership content knowledge?

Research question 6. How does the management curriculum, as reported by program faculty, provide students with experiences to apply leadership content knowledge?

Research question 7. Are there any other elements of the college experience that may prepare students for leadership?

Definitions

Table 5

Definitions of Terms

Elements of the College Experience	Leadership content knowledge and application simulations as designed in curriculum
Four year college	An accredited institution offering a course of study leading to a Bachelor of Science in Business Administration degree.
Leadership	"Inducing followers to act for certain goals that represent the values and the motivations—the wants and needs, the

aspirations and expectations—of both leaders and followers" (Burns, 1978, p. 381)

Leadership Behaviors

Challenge the Process: Leading involves change. Change requires altering existing processes. Leaders must be willing to take risks when challenging the status quo.

Inspire a Shared Vision: Ability to persuade others that the leader's goals and visions for the future are the same as theirs.

Enable Others to Act: Effective leaders cultivate collaboration and trust. Leaders and followers are trusted and supported in their efforts.

Model the Way: Leader sets the example of required behavior within the organization. Also helps define climate and culture of the organization by providing an example

	Encourage the Heart: Leader uses intrinsic rewards to motivate individuals within the organization. Recognition, achievement, advancement, growth, and increased responsibility are among the tools leaders use to make members of the organization feel valued and spur them on to greater achievements.
Leadership Content Knowledge	Subject information within the curriculum specifically focusing on leadership
Management Curriculum	Curriculum of all courses leading to a 4 year degree from the School of Management
Program Faculty	All full-time faculty in the School of Management.
Traditional format	A college program of study comprised of 15 week semesters, with 45 faculty contact hours per 3 credit-hour course.

Design of the Study

This study applied a single case study design. The purpose of the study was to describe how students and faculty perceive the college's management program develops the students' leadership knowledge and skills. This study also described how the elements of the program's curriculum are intended to help students meet employers' expectations for leadership abilities in the candidates they consider for employment.

Yin (2009) said "that case studies are the preferred method when (a) "how" or "why" questions are being posed, (b) the investigator has little control over events, and (c) the focus is on a contemporary phenomenon within a real-life context"(p. 2).

All of these conditions were true in this case, and the researcher was not going to intervene in any way with the contemporary phenomenon being studied. The phenomenon of a business program preparing students in terms of leadership development to meet employers' expectations is a contemporary, increasingly important aspect of a business student's academic preparation.

According to Yin (2009), there are four tests that are used to establish the quality of social research such as case studies (p. 40). These four tests are addressed in the design of this case study. The four tests are: construct validity, internal validity, external validity, and reliability.

Construct Validity

Yin (2009) defined construct validity as "identifying correct operational measures for the concepts being measured" (p. 40). To do this the researcher must define the specific concepts being examined and relate them to the original objectives of the study (p. 42). The researcher should then "identify operational measures that match the concepts (preferably citing published studies that make the same matches)" (p. 42).

Yin (2009) identified three tactics that establish construct validity when doing case studies. These are: using multiple sources of evidence, establishing a chain of evidence, and having informants review the draft case study report.

Using multiple sources of evidence in data collection can be a major source of strength, according to Yin (2009). The author notes that "case studies using multiple sources of evidence were rated more highly, in terms of their overall quality, than those that relied on only single sources of information" (p. 117). In this case study the researcher will collect evidence from individuals using three separate data collection tools. The three different instruments that will be utilized are a student interview guide, a faculty interview guide, and a survey. Thus, complementary lines of inquiry will be used in this study to help us understand strategies used in this business program to help students develop their leadership skills.

Establishing a chain of evidence was the second tactic for bolstering construct validity listed by Yin (2009). The reader of the case study should be able "to follow the derivation of evidence from initial research questions to ultimate case study conclusions. Moreover, the external observer should be able to trace the steps in either direction" (p. 122), from research question to conclusion and back. Yin describes the process of establishing and maintaining the chain of evidence as being similar to a criminal investigation. The process should leave no doubt that the evidence presented in the case study is the same as the evidence collected by the researcher. It should be complete, with "no original evidence lost through carelessness or bias" (p. 123.) All evidence must be given due consideration when deliberating the case facts. In this study all interview transcripts will be reviewed with the respective interviewee to ensure accuracy and completeness.

In this case study the survey, or SLPI (Kouzes and Posner, 2002), was derived from the conceptual framework (Kouzes & Posner, 2002) based on five leadership behaviors. This framework will provide a lens for examining student accounts of their self-perceptions of their leadership development. Additional open-ended interview questions will be incorporated into the study design due to the exploratory nature of the additional information sought. According to Creswell (2009), "a researcher may want to both generalize the findings to a population as well as develop a detailed view of the meaning of a phenomenon or concept for individuals" (p. 18). Such is the case in this study. By combining research methods, this study seeks to better understand the process of preparing students to meet prospective employers' expectations for candidates' leadership development.

Yin (2009) posited that the third method of increasing construct validity was to have informants review the case study reports for accuracy. The informants do not need to agree with the researchers' conclusions, but they should agree over the facts that led to the conclusions. Moreover, the author noted that the review process can lead to the recall of additional facts, and possible clarifications of some facts already recorded. The new or revised information can then be incorporated into subsequent revisions of the draft, leading to an improved manuscript. The improved accuracy of the revisions serves to increase the construct validity of the study. Not all reinterpretations of the facts on the part of the informants need to be included in the revision; the researcher is entitled to their own interpretation (p. 183). The researcher in this study will utilize member checking as recommended by Yin.

Internal Validity

The second test of a case study's validity is internal validity. This is a concern when the researcher is attempting to establish causality. Some of the tactics used include pattern matching, explanation building, addressing rival explanations, and using logic models (p. 43). This case study will not attempt to establish causality, rather it seeks only to observe and describe, and hence internal validity will not be addressed by the researcher.

External Validity

The third test is external validity. The concern of this test is the determination of whether it can be generalized to a larger population. Yin (2009) maintained that critics argued that single case studies offer a poor basis for generalizing. In fact, single case studies lend themselves to analytic generalization, rather than the statistical generalizations to other settings. Yin admonished that analytic generalizations are not automatic; rather their theories must be tested in one or more subsequent case studies where the same results could be observed.

The survey data recorded in this single-case study was viewed and analyzed through the lens of the five leadership behaviors as developed by Kouzes and Posner (2002). The complementary data from the open-ended interview questions are intended to provide greater depth of understanding, as recommended by Creswell (2009).

Reliability of the Design

The fourth test of the rigor of a case study, according to Yin (2009), involves the reliability of the design. Yin(2009) asserted "the goal of reliability is to minimize the errors and biases in a study" (p. 45). When successful, later researchers should be able to replicate the study, its findings, and its conclusions.

According to Yin (2009), an important step in achieving reliability is documenting all of the study's procedures. When thorough, the record of procedures allows the researcher, as well as subsequent researchers, to repeat the original work, arriving at the same conclusions. Yin (2009) recommends making the procedures as operational as possible to most readily facilitate replication. The author concluded by advising that it was best to conduct and record research with easy replication in mind. This level of transparency raises the perceived quality of the research design.

A valuable tool for documenting the case study's procedures is a case study protocol. Yin maintained that the protocol "keeps you targeted on the topic of the case study" (p. 81), as well as "forcing you to anticipate several problems, including the way that the case study reports are to be completed" (p. 82). Yin (2009) advised that the protocol should contain four main sections. The first section is the project overview, followed by the field procedures, the case study questions, and finally, a guide for the case study report. The researcher in this study will follow and report the research protocol. The procedures described in this chapter constitute the preliminary phase of the case study protocol, with the remainder will be reported following the data collection activities.

The second tactic described by Yin (2009) is to develop a case-study database as a way of organizing and documenting the data collected. The data collected is divided into two categories; the data or evidentiary base, and the report of the investigator.

The data or evidentiary base is comprised of four components, as recommended by Yin (2009, p. 119). The components are the notes, documents, tabular materials, and narratives.

Tabular materials include the quantitative data generated from the administration of the S-LPI to the student participants in the study. Frequencies and other data generated from the qualitative portions of the study were also listed here. Qualitative portions consist of faculty and student interviews whose open ended questions were guided by the conceptual framework described earlier.

Population and Sample

The Participating College

The private, four-year college in the study is an urban school with an emphasis on career preparation. Within this college, the four year programs in the school of management include programs leading to bachelors' degree in management with concentrations in general management, marketing, hospitality management, entertainment management, and fashion merchandizing. The population is thus comprised of the college and other similar career focused colleges.

Student and Faculty Samples

According to Yin (2009) a single-case study involves capturing a common example, one that is typical or representative of a larger population. According to Creswell (2005), a purposeful sample in qualitative research is desirable and occurs when investigators select individuals and sites that are likely to help them to understand the characteristics of the phenomenon they are studying. A purposive sample of 80 business students in their final year at a private four-year college will be selected because they are representative of the reference group. In addition to exhibiting characteristics similar to the reference group, these students are available to the researcher. According to Creswell (2005), the researcher can select participants because they are ready and available to take part in the study.

Currently, the participating college in this study has a total enrollment of 753 students; 199 men and 554 women. The School of Management has 205 students enrolled in the Bachelor of Science in Management program. These enrolled students have the options of concentrations in Management, Marketing, Hospitality Management, and Entertainment Management, and Fashion Merchandizing. With regard to ethnicity, the students at college are classified as follows: 189 Black

Non-Hispanic, 89 Hispanic, 16 Asian-Pacific Islander, 31 American Indian/Alaskan Native, 353 White Non-Hispanic, and 71 race unknown.

Demographic information describing those students from the School of Management in the final year of the program leading to a Bachelor of Science in Management falls along lines similar to the demographics for students of the college as a whole. These final year students were available to complete the SLPI after completion of final exams in December.

Student interview participants were randomly selected from the population of 38 survey respondents. They were interviewed about their self-perceptions in the area of leadership development, specifically as it relates to meeting employers' expectations for candidates leadership abilities.

Currently, the School of Management has 8 full-time faculty members combined with a list of adjunct instructors that can be changed to reflect variations in enrollment. The 8 full-time faculty members are responsible for creation and revision of the curricula for the courses that they teach. The full-time faculty is comprised of 3 men and 5 women. All 8 of the full-time faculty members within the school of management were asked to be interviewed regarding the elements of their curricula intended to foster leadership development among students.

In summary, the researcher chose the School of Management at a small, private college in a northeastern state as the unit of analysis for his study because it shared the essential characteristics with a larger reference group of business students at similar small, career focused colleges. These students will soon be serving businesses, and attempting to meet their expectations for leadership development. The eight full-time faculty members from the School of Management were interviewed regarding the elements of the curriculum intended to foster students' leadership development. 38 of the 85 students in the final year of a program leading to a Bachelor of Science in Management completed the SLPI

(Kouzes and Posner, 2002) to establish a baseline measurement of leadership behaviors as seen through the lens of students' self-perceptions. Finally a group of 10 students randomly selected from the SLPI group were interviewed regarding the curriculum's emphasis on their leadership development, specifically as it relates to meeting employers' expectations for candidates leadership abilities.

Data Collection Instruments

This single case study was conducted in three phases. First, 38 of the 85 students in their final year agreed to complete the SLPI (Kouzes & Posner, 2002). Then, a group of 10 students, randomly selected from the SLPI group were interviewed about their self perceptions of their leadership development, specifically the extent to which the management curriculum has assisted in their leadership development. Second, the full time faculty members from the School of Management at the small private college in a northeastern state were interviewed about the elements of the curriculum intended to foster students' leadership development. The student and faculty interviews were designed by the researcher, reviewed by the researcher's advisor and pilot tested. These three sources of data provide complementary lines of inquiry, allowing for triangulation and providing greater depth of understanding, as recommended by Creswell (2005).

Protection of Human Subjects

The human subjects review process was completed as required by the University of Hartford Human Subjects Committee and the Human Subjects Committee of the college in this study (Appendix A).

Students were contacted by email. Upon receiving the email, students were asked to complete the attached informed consent form prior to completing the survey. Interviewees (both students and faculty) were presented with the informed consent form prior to the administration of the interview.

According to Creswell (2002), it is important to protect the identity of the informants when gathering, analyzing, and reporting data. The confidentiality of participants was maintained throughout this study. Materials (online survey) were not coded in any identifiable way. All of the study participants and the school were assigned numeric pseudonyms. All data was reported either in aggregate, our using pseudonyms. Strict confidentiality was maintained. No personally identifying information was collected. All digital files were saved in a secure computer and paper files will be stored in a locked file cabinet in the researcher's office. Each file is accessible only to the researcher and his advisor.

The data collected from this investigation will be kept for a period of five years, to allow for data verification and confirmation of results and analysis (American Psychological Association, 2010, p. 12). After five years, all data and analysis (digital and paper) will be destroyed.

Data Collection

A three-method approach will be used to answer the research questions; student volunteers were asked to complete an on-line version of the SLPI, ten students randomly selected from the SLPI group were interviewed, and full-time faculty from the School of Management were interviewed. Interviews were held in the conference room adjacent the faculty offices.

Data Analysis

Yin (2009) wrote of four general strategies for data analysis in case studies. The third of these he called *Using both qualitative and quantitative data* (p. 132). The author wrote of case studies with substantial amounts of quantitative data subjected to statistical analysis, that if qualitative data remains "central to the entire case study, you will have successfully followed a strong analytic strategy" (p. 132). Such is the goal of the data analysis in this study. The student SLPI results will be loaded into Excel, which will generate statistics including frequencies, means, and standard deviations. These statistics should in no way detract from the centrality of the qualitative data generated by the student and faculty interviews.

The qualitative data generated by both the student and faculty interviews were extracted from the transcriptions of the interviews and the subsequent open-coding. According to Creswell (2005), coding involves "taking text data or pictures gathered during data collection, segmenting sentences (or paragraphs) or images into categories, and labeling those categories with a term" (p. 186). This process will be used in the analysis of the interview transcriptions.

Table 6 shows how data collection and analysis are organized in relation to the research questions.

Table 6

Data source and Analysis Chart

Research Question	Data Source	Analysis
Research question 1. What are business students' self-reports about their leadership behaviors as articulated by Kouzes and Posner and measured by the S-LPI (Kouzes & Posner, 2002).	(Student LPI) 30 Behavior-Based Questions Survey	Frequency, Mean and Standard Deviation
Research question 1a. What are business students' self-reports about the leadership behavior Model the Way.	(Student LPI) 6 Behavior-Based Questions Survey 1, 6, 11, 16, 21, 26	Frequency, Mean and Standard Deviation

Research question 1b. What are business students' self-reports about the leadership behavior Inspire a Shared Vision.	(Student LPI) 6 Behavior-Based Questions Survey 2, 7, 12, 17, 22, 27	Frequency, Mean and Standard Deviation
Research question 1c. What are the business students' self-reports about the leadership behavior Challenge the Process.	(Student LPI) 6 Behavior-Based Questions Survey 3, 8, 13, 18, 23, 28	Frequency, Mean and Standard Deviation
Research question 1d. What are business students' self-reports about the leadership behavior Enable Others to Act.	(Student LPI) 6 Behavior-Based Questions Survey 4, 9, 14, 19, 24, 29	Frequency, Mean and Standard Deviation
Research question 1e. What are business students' self-reports about the leadership behavior Encourage the Heart.	(Student LPI) 6 Behavior-Based Questions Survey 5, 10,15, 20, 25, 30	Frequency, Mean and Standard Deviation Open Coding
Research question 2. What are business students' self-reports about their preparedness to meet potential employers' expectations of a candidate's leadership development?	Student Interviews	Open Coding

Research question 3. What are business students' perceptions about the elements of the curriculum that contributed most to their leadership development?	Student Interviews	Open Coding
Research question 4. What are business students' perceptions about other elements of the college experience that may prepare them for leadership?	Student Interviews	Open Coding
Research question 5. How does the management curriculum, as reported by program faculty, help students acquire leadership content knowledge?	Faculty Interviews	Open Coding
Research question 6. How does the management curriculum, as reported by program faculty, provide students with experiences to apply leadership content knowledge?	Faculty Interviews	Open Coding

Research question 7. Are there any other elements of the college experience that may prepare students for leadership?	Faculty Interviews	Open Coding

Limitations of the Study

There are numerous limitations to this study. Conducting this study at one small college in a northeastern state, and looking at only one senior class of students limits the generalizability of the findings. The use of perceptions and self-reported data also has inherent limitations. Despite every effort to avoid it, researcher bias may be present, due to the researcher's employment at the school being studied. Finally, the interview guides have not been used in a previous study.

Chapter 4: Presentation of the Findings

Introduction

This chapter reports the findings for this single case study of student and faculty perceptions about the elements of the curriculum that foster leadership development at the school of management in a small four-year college in a northeastern state. To begin, there is a brief review of the research design and methodology. This is followed by a review of the research site along with a description of the faculty and students found therein. The remainder of the chapter presents the findings according to the primary research question and the five sub-research questions associated with the leadership behaviors as described in the conceptual framework (Kouzes & Posner, 2002). The quantitative data from the School of Management SLPI is presented along with baseline data reported by

Posner (2010). This is followed by qualitative data from faculty and student interviews. The chapter ends with a summary of the key findings.

Study Methodology

The methodology for this single case study examined how students enrolled in their final year of a Bachelor of Science degree program and faculty in the participating school of management perceive the program develops the students' leadership skills. The conceptual framework that guided this study was drawn from Kouzes and Posner's (2002) five exemplary leadership behaviors. A mixed method approach was used to collect data, and this study proceeded in two complementary ways. The researcher examined students' perceptions of their leadership behaviors along with faculty accounts of the program elements pertaining to leadership. In the first, Kouzes and Posner's (2002) student version of the Leadership Practices Inventory (S-LPI) was administered to students ($N =$ 38). The self-reported accounts of leadership development by students provided baseline information about the extent of their leadership content knowledge as defined by the study's conceptual framework. From the SLPI group, a randomly selected sample of students ($N = 10$) responded to additional interview questions. The interviews solicited their accounts of where during their education they learned about leadership and where during their education they had the opportunity to apply this content knowledge. Faculty interviews ($N = 8$) focused on the elements of the curriculum and overall college experience intended to foster students' leadership development.

The SLPI consisted of thirty web-based questions categorizing the students' self-perceptions of their leadership behaviors into five dimensions: Modeling the Way, Inspiring a Shared Vision, Challenging the Process, Enabling Others to Act, and Encouraging the Heart. The student responses to the SLPI indicated whether they (1) "Never," (2) "Rarely," (3) "Sometimes," (4) "Often," or (5) "Very

Frequently" used the five leadership practices. The students accessed the instrument via a link embedded in a participant specific email. The *SLPI online* website tabulated the survey data and produced inferential statistics.

The qualitative instruments used in this study consisted of two sets of semi-structured interview questions. Participant responses were recorded and transcribed. The students completed an eight question interview that included 5 questions specifically pertaining to the leadership practices as described by Kouzes and Posner. The School of Management faculty completed a 7 question interview which contained 5 questions specifically pertaining to the same leadership behaviors. All qualitative data was open-coded with code frequencies entered into a Word table.

Research Site and Participant Characteristics

The private, four-year college in the study is an urban school with an emphasis on career preparation. A survey link was emailed to the 85 school of management students that had earned ninety or more credits. Thirty eight of the eighty five seniors (44.7%) completed the survey, with ten participants randomly selected from the thirty eight participating in the qualitative student interviews. Seven of the eight full-time faculty members then participated in the faculty interviews.

Findings

Finding 1.0. The findings presented in Table 7 are the aggregated results of the SLPI, which address the first research question: What are business students' self-reports about their leadership behaviors as articulated by Kouzes and Posner and measured by the S-LPI? Norming data compiled by Posner (2010) in a meta-analysis of studies conducted from 2007 to 2009 and displaying the SLPI results from college students ($N = 983$) is included in the table as a comparative reference.

Results of Student Survey

Table 7

SLPI Means and Standard Deviations for School of Management (SOM) Seniors
(N = 38) compared with Means and Standard Deviations for College Students
(N=979) in Posner's Meta-analysis(PM)

Leadership Practice	SOM Mean	SOM Standard Deviation	PM MEAN	PM Standard Deviation
Model the Way	22.6	3.4	22.12	3.3
Inspire a Shared Vision	23.2	2.4	21.81	4.03
Challenge the Process	23.2	2.9	21.51	3.71
Enable Others to Act	24.5	2.8	24.0	3.07
Encourage the Heart	24	3.1	22.71	4.05

The mean for the SOM responses to the questions related to the behavior
Model the Way was 22.6 out of a possible 30, which was comparable to the Posner
norming data of 22.12. The dispersion was also comparable at 3.4 for the SOM

and 3.3 for the Posner group. SOM students' responses to those questions pertaining to the behavior Inspire a Shared Vision resulted in a mean score of 23.2, as compared to 21.81 for the PM group. There was also a larger difference in the variability of responses, with the standard deviation of the SOM students at 2.4, while the standard deviation PM students was 4.03. The leadership practice Challenge the Process data indicated that the self perceptions of the SOM students resulted in a higher mean (23.2 vs. 21.51) and less variability (2.9 vs. 3.71) than the PM group. The mean associated with the practice Enable Others to Act were comparable with the SOM students' results averaging 24.5 with a standard deviation of 2.8, while the larger PM group averaged 24.0 with a standard deviation of 3.07. The fifth category of leadership practices, Encourage the Heart, yielded comparable results with means of 24.0 and 22.71 for the SOM students and the PM group respectively. Variability was also comparable with the SOM standard deviation of 3.1 and the PM standard deviation at 4.05.

Reviewing the data in table 7, it is apparent that students perceptions at the participating school are equal to or exceeds those of the Posner norming group in all categories. Three of the categories, Inspire, Challenge, and Encourage appear to be especially strong program areas when compared to the norming group. More detailed examination of the responses by the students participating in this study follow in a description and analysis of Table 8.

Table 8 breaks down the data displayed in table 7, showing how students in the participating school answered never, rarely, sometimes, often, and very frequently in response to the instrument's 30 questions. These questions, along with the numbers of student responses are grouped by major Kouzes and Posner leadership behaviors.

Table 8

Student Responses to SLPI Questions Grouped by Behavior

Behavior/Question	Never	Rarely	Sometimes	Often	Very Frequently
Model the Way					
1. Sets personal example	0	3	6	14	15
6. Aligns others with principles and standards	0	0	8	20	10
11. Follows through on promises	0	0	8	20	10
16. Gets feedback about actions	0	2	4	20	12
21. Builds consensus on values	0	0	2	21	15
26. Talks about values and principles	0	3	8	25	2
Inspire a Shared Vision					
2. Looks ahead and communicates future	0	2	7	20	9
7. Describes ideal capabilities	0	5	5	20	8
12. Talks about vision of the future	0	1	4	9	24
17. Shows others how their interests can be realized	0	0	11	19	8
22. Paints "big picture" of group aspirations	0	0	5	16	17

27. Communicates purpose and meaning	0	2	3	23	10

Challenge the Process

3.Develops skills and abilities	0	2	18	7	11
8. Helps others take risks	0	0	1	7	30
13. Searches outside organization for innovative ways to improve	0	0	1	26	11
18. Asks "What can we learn"	2	6	11	13	6
23. Makes certain that goals, plans, and milestones are set	2	3	6	23	4
28. Takes initiative in experimenting	0	1	10	15	12

Enable Others to Act

4. Fosters cooperative relationships	0	1	16	16	5
9. Actively listens	0	1	4	9	24
14. Treats others with respect	0	2	18	11	7
19. Supports decisions other people make	0	0	1	7	30
24. Gives people choice about how to do their work	0	2	5	16	15
29. Provides leadership opportunities	0	1	12	15	10

Encourage the Heart

5. Praises people	1	1	10	18	8

10. Encourages others	2	3	10	15	8
15. Provides support and appreciation	4	2	11	15	6
20. Publicly recognizes alignment with values	2	2	10	19	5
25. Celebrates accomplishments	1	5	9	17	6
30. Creatively recognizes people	3	3	3	20	9

As shown in table 8, there are 6 sub-behaviors that comprise each of the 5 leadership practices. The student responses indicate their perception of the management program's specific areas of strength, as well as areas that may benefit from curriculum revision. The results in each of the 5 Kouzes and Posner categories will now be described.

Finding 1a. Model the Way

The analysis of School of Management students' responses to questions in the category Model the Way show a clustering of responses in the *often* and *very frequently* columns. None of the participants answered *never* and only 8 responded *rarely* when responding to any of the six questions in this category. Students' responses to questions 6, 11, and 21 excluded the use of the *never* and *rarely* ratings. The overall lowest scoring question in this category was question 26, *talks about values and principals*, and it prompted 3 *rarely* and 8 *sometimes* responses, with 27 of the students opting for *often* or *very frequently*. Responses to question

1: *sets personal example,* and question 16: *gets feedback about actions,* included 3 *rarely* and 6 *sometimes* for the former and 2 *rarely* and 4 *sometimes* for the latter.

The sizable majority of students report ample opportunities to perform all six of the Kouzes and Posner sub-behaviors. A small number in each category indicated only being able to perform such behaviors sometimes or rarely. Building Consensus on Values in particular emerged as an area of emphasis within the program, while Talking about Principles and Values emerged as an area that could be strengthened.

Finding 1b. Inspire a Shared Vision

Questions categorized under the leadership practice Inspire a Shared Vision included number 2; Looks Ahead and Communicates Future. Twenty of the SOM students responded *often,* making this the most common response. The second most frequent response was *very frequently* with 9 responses, followed by *sometimes* with 7, *rarely* with 2, and *never* with 0. The responses to question 7, Describes Ideal Capabilities, were similar to question 2. Twenty of the participants answered *often,* followed by *very frequently* with 8 responses, followed by *sometimes* with 5, *rarely* with 5, and *never* with 0.

The responses to question 12, Talks about Vision of the Future, along with question 22, Paints "big picture" of Group Aspirations, were greatest in the *very frequently* column (24 and 17 respectively). Question 12 had only 1 *rarely* response along with 4 *sometimes*, and 9 indicating *often*. Question 22 also garnered 5 *sometimes* and 16 *often* responses.

Survey question 17, Shows Others How Their Interests can be Realized, indicated an area of confidence with none of the respondents choosing *never* or *rarely* and 11 choosing *sometimes*, 19 choosing *often*, and 8 indicating *very frequently*. The remaining question in the category was number 27, Communicates Purpose and Meaning. The most frequent response to this question was *often* with 23, followed by *very frequently* with 10, *sometimes* with 3, and *rarely* with 2.

The sub-behaviors in this category all reflected the relative strength of the program, with the majority of students indicating experience with the practices. Talks about Vision of the Future was the strongest sub-behavior, while Shows Others how their Interests can be realized proved to represent the greatest opportunity for improvement.

Finding 1c. Challenge the Process

The 6 questions describing the practice Challenging the Process included 2 lower scoring areas: number 18, *Asks "what can we learn",* and number 23, *makes certain that goals, plans, and milestones are set".* The responses for number 18 include 2 *never*, 6 *rarely*, 11 *sometimes*, 13 *often*, and 16 *very frequently*. Similarly, the responses for question 23 include 2 *never*, 3 *rarely*, 6 *sometimes*, 23 *often*, and 4 *very frequently*.

The sub-behavior Help Others Take Risks was practiced very frequently or often by nearly all of the participants, indicating that this was an area of strength for the School of Management. The student responses to the question related to the sub-behavior Asks "What Can We Learn" indicated an area of leadership development that represents a growth opportunity.

Finding 1d. Enable Others to Act

The practice Enable Others to Act is notable in that none of the SOM students answered *never* to any of the questions in this category. Responses to question 4, *fosters cooperative relationships,* included 1 *rarely*, 16 *sometimes*, 16 *often*, and 5 *very frequently*. The students responded even more positively to question 9, *actively listens,* with 1 responding *rarely*, 4 *sometimes*, 9 *often*, and 24 *very frequently*. They were somewhat less affirmative with replies to question 14, *treats others with respect*, with the majority (18) responding *sometimes.* The balance of the responses was as follows: 2 *rarely*, 11 *often*, and 7 *very frequently*. When answering question 19, *supports decisions other people make,* 30 students responded with *very frequently,* 7 replied *often*, and 1 said *sometimes. Gives people choice about how to do their work* was question 24, and the SOM students answered with 2 choosing *rarely,* 5 *sometimes,* 16 *provides leadership opportunities,* were as follows: 1 *rarely,* 10 sometimes, 18 *often*, and 8 *very frequently.*

The majority of students report adequate opportunity to practice the sub-behaviors in this category. A sub-behavior that reflected program strength was Supports Decisions Other People Make, with all but one students responding *very frequently* or *often*. Treats Others with Respect emerged as the primary sub-behavior that could be strengthened.

Finding 1e. Encourage the Heart

The responses to the questions in this section included more *never* choices than those of any other leadership practice. Question 5, *praises people,* elicited 1 *never* response, in addition to 1 *rarely,* 10 that replied *sometimes*, 18 *often*, and 8 who replied *very frequently.* A very similar distribution of responses occurred on the next five questions in the category; *encourages others, provides support and appreciation, publicly recognizes alignment with values, celebrates accomplishments, and creatively recognizes people.*

Provides Support and Appreciation was the weakest sub-behavior in this category, and as such represents a growth opportunity. Student self-reports about the sub-behavior Praises People indicated the area of greatest strength in this category.

Students Interview Responses

Finding 2.0. Students (*n=10*) were randomly selected from the SLPI group and interviewed by the researcher. The interviews were electronically recorded (mp3 format) and transcribed. The transcriptions were subsequently open-coded with frequencies entered into a series of tables. The first interview question mirrored research question 2; *what are business students' self-reports about their preparedness to meet potential employers' expectations of a candidate's leadership development?* Responses by all ten participants were affirmative, ranging from "pretty well, I think I can do it" to "above and beyond". Five of the ten replied simply that they were "very well" prepared. The remaining responses were "better than before college", "confident, I feel that I can do it" and "as prepared as I can be". The students' responses are displayed in table 9 below.

Table 9

Student responses to: How well prepared are you to meet potential employers' expectations of a candidate's leadership development?

Student 1	Better than before college
Student 2	Above and beyond
Student 3	Pretty prepared, I network with experienced people
Student 4	As prepared as I can be
Student 5,7,8,9,10	Very well or pretty well
Student 6	Pretty confident, I feel I can do it

Finding 3.0. The next interview question addresses research question 3, *What are business students' perceptions about the elements of the curriculum that contributed most to their leadership development?* The responses to this question ranged widely, with Managerial Leadership being this most frequently cited with 5 responses. The capstone course, Strategic Management, garnered 2 responses. Organizational Behavior and the Entertainment Management Practicum also were

each mentioned by 2 students. The rest of the courses were Public Speaking, Psychology, Human Resource Management, and Hospitality Law, each with 1 response. There were 3 responses that were not course titles. The three non-course responses were Being a Student Leader, Self Learning, and Managing the Spot, with each being mentioned once. Table 10 below summarizes the students' responses.

Table 10

Student responses to: What are your perceptions about the elements of the curriculum that contributed most to your leadership development?

Managerial Leadership	5
Strategic Management	2
Organizational Behavior	2
Entertainment Management Practicum	2
Public Speaking	1
Psychology	1
Human Resource Management	1
Hospitality Law	1
Being a Student Leader	1
Self Learning	1
Managing the "Venue"	1

Both students and faculty were asked questions about each of Kouzes and Posner's 5 leadership practices. Responses were compared to see if the intentions of faculty, through their curriculum design, were recalled by the students. Table 11 displays the responses and frequencies of both groups to the interview questions. Responses are grouped first by course, and second by intra-course activities.

Table 11

Comparison of Student Reponses to Research Question 3 and Faculty Responses to Research Question 5, by Leadership Practice

Courses

Practice	*Students*	*Faculty*
Model the Way	Managerial Leadership 2	Management 3
	Public Speaking 1	Intro to Business 1
	Principals of Management 1	Entertainment Business 1
	Introduction to Hospitality 1	Strategic Management 1
	Many Classes 5	Many Classes 1
	None 2	Venue Management 1

		Events Management 1
		Concert Production 1
Inspire a Shared Vision	Managerial Leadership 5	Management 2
	Public Speaking 5	Public Speaking 1
	Organizational Behavior 2	Negotiation 1
	Entertainment Practicum 1	Venue Management 1
	None 1	Events Management 1
		Concert Production 1
		Textiles 1

Challenge the Process	Managerial Leadership 3	Principals of Management 3
	Organizational Behavior 2	Entertainment Practicum 2
	Public Speaking 1	Strategic Management 1
	Intro to Hospitality 1	Venue Management 1
	Operations Management 1	Events Management 1
	Principles of Marketing 1	Concert Production 1
	Macroeconomics 1	
Enable Others to Act	Managerial Leadership 4	Management 2
	Organizational Behavior	Venue Management

	3	1
	Principles of Marketing 2	Events Management 1
	International Management 1	Concert Production 1
	Food and Beverage Ops 1	
	Business Law 1	
	Psychology 1	
Encourage the Heart	Managerial Leadership 5	Principles of Management 1
	Organizational Behavior 1	Venue Management 1
	Business Law 1	Events Management 1

		Concert Production 1
Instructional Strategies		
Model the Way	Group Work 2	Case Studies/Simulations 4
	Presentations 1	Faculty Model 1
Inspire a Shared Vision	None mentioned	Group Work 2
		Case Studies 1
Challenge the Process	Group Work 3	Case Studies 1
Enable Others to Act	None Mentioned	Hands on 2
		Case Studies 1
Encourage the Heart	Group Work 1	Fashion Show 1

		Hands on
		2

Finding 3.a. In the first of these questions students were asked, which elements of the curriculum taught you about the leadership behavior Model the Way? Correspondingly, only 1 student recalled Principles of Management as being a source of leadership content knowledge, although all ten had completed the course. Moreover, there were no other courses cited by both groups. A total of 5 students said the topic was addressed in many classes. Two of the students interviewed said that Managerial Leadership was a source of this knowledge, while one student cited Public Speaking and another cited Introduction to Hospitality. Two students said that none of their courses were sources of information about Modeling the Way.

Finding 3.b. When asked about the leadership practice Inspire a Shared Vision, 5 students mentioned Public Speaking, while none of the students interviewed mentioned Principals of Management. t Managerial Leadership was recalled by 5 students, and Organizational Behavior was recalled by 2. One student thought the Entertainment Practicum was a source of this knowledge, and 1 other student said that none of the courses delivered this content.

Finding 3.c. In the third leadership practice, Challenge the Process, 1 student cited Principals of Management as a source of related content knowledge. Two students mentioned Organizational Behavior, and 3 said Managerial Leadership. The following course were each cited by 1 student; Public Speaking, Introduction to Hospitality, Operations Management, Principles of Marketing, and Macroeconomics.

Finding 3.d. Enable Others to Act was the topic of the fourth set of interview questions. There were no points of agreement between faculty and students in this section. Student responses included 4 that mentioned Managerial Leadership, 3 that said Organizational Behavior, and 2 that cited Principles of Marketing as the courses that taught them the content knowledge associated with this practice. Also, each of the following were mentioned by 1 student; International Management, Food and Beverage Operations, Business Law, and Psychology.

Finding 3.e. The last set of interview questions among those pertaining to courses that teach the 5 leadership behaviors asked about the practice Encourage the Heart. Student responses included 5 that mentioned Managerial Leadership, 1 that mentioned Organizational Behavior, and 1 that said Business Law.

The next section of table 11 displays faculty and students' instructional strategy responses to the same interview questions. These activities were cited by either students or faculty, or both, as central to teaching the leadership content knowledge specified in the interview questions. These responses were not course specific; rather the interviewees felt the activities, possibly utilized in multiple courses, were primarily responsible for the transfer of the content knowledge.

Two students said that group work had taught them this practice, while one cited class presentations.

While none of the students could cite an instructional strategy that taught them the practice Inspire a Shared Vision,

Three students mentioned group work as an activity that helped them learn about the practice Challenge the Process, while   Students offered no responses in the category Enable Others to Act.

Only one student response noted group work as the source of learning about the practice Encourage the Heart.

Finding 4.0. The final student interview questions asked about other elements of the college experience that prepare students for leadership. In response, three students mentioned that the DECA case study competition team was an element of the college experience that helped to prepare students for leadership. One Student cited MEISA, the Music and Entertainment Industry Student Association. Three students mentioned the Student Government Association, while one said that being a RA (dormitory resident assistant) was something that would prepare students for leadership. Two students cited internships as contributing to students' preparedness for leadership. The above responses were matched by varying levels of agreement by faculty in Finding 7.0.

Other responses by students not mentioned by faculty in Finding 7.0 conclude this section. One student also mentioned being a peer mentor along with being a student ambassador. Another student cited membership in the Massachusetts Lodging Association as something that can contribute to leadership preparedness. Another student said working in the entertainment management venue should be listed here as well.

Finding 5.a. The seven full-time faculty members were asked how does the management curriculum help students acquire leadership content knowledge about the behavior Model the Way? Faculty responses included 3 of the 8 citing Principles of Management as a course that teaches leadership. Those 3 recounted how the course is structured around the 4 functions of management; plan, organize, lead and control. This course is required of all bachelors' degree students in the school of management. Leading, according to faculty, is discussed at length. One faculty member said that Introduction to Business was a source of leadership content knowledge. Four entertainment management courses were specified by a single faculty member: Entertainment Management, Events Management, Venue Management, and Concert Production. Strategic Management was cited on 1 occasion, by the program chair. The program chair also stated that content knowledge related to modeling the way is "woven throughout the curriculum".

Finding 5.b. When asked about the leadership practice Inspire a Shared Vision, Public Speaking was recalled by 1 faculty member. Negotiations, Event Management, Venue Management, Concert Production, and Textiles were each mentioned once by faculty.

Finding 5.c. In response to the question about the third leadership practice, Challenge the Process, 3 faculty members again cited Principles of Management as a source of related content knowledge. One faculty member cited Strategic Management and 2 faculty members mentioned the Entertainment Practicum. Events Management, Venue Management, and Concert Production were each mentioned by 1 faculty.

Finding 5.d. Enable Others to Act was the topic of the fourth set of interview questions. Faculty responses included 2 for Principles of Management and 1 each for Events Management, Venue Management, and Concert Production.

Finding 5.e. The last faculty interview question among those pertaining to courses that teach the 5 leadership behaviors asked about the practice Encourage the Heart. Faculty responses included 1 each for Principles of Management, Events Management, Venue Management, and Concert Production.

Among the instructional strategies, four of the faculty members interviewed felt that the practice Model the Way was best demonstrated through case studies and like simulations. One faculty member also felt that the most effective method of providing instruction about this practice was by personally providing an example, or in other words, model the way herself.

When responding to the question addressing Inspire a Shared Vision, 2 of the faculty interviewed mentioned group work, and one cited case studies as effective methods of transferring the related content knowledge.

When answering the question regarding the practice Challenge the Process, one faculty member said that case studies were their preferred method of teaching this practice.

The responses for instructional strategies that help teach the practice Enable Others to Act included 2 faculty members that responded with anything "hands on", and one that admonished that case studies were most effective.

Instructional strategies related to the practice Encourage the Heart included 2 members of the school of management faculty that replied "hands on", and one that said that working at the annual Fashion Show would teach this practice.

Finding 6.0. The school of management faculty was asked how the curriculum provided students with experiences to apply the leadership content knowledge that had been provided over the course of the program. Responses are displayed in Table 12, in the order that they were interviewed.

Table 12

Faculty responses to research question 6, How does the management curriculum provide students with experiences to apply leadership content knowledge?

Faculty member 1, 2, 6	Group projects, group work
	DECA
Faculty member 3	It is all hands on
Faculty member 4	They lead by doing, hands on
Faculty member 5	Managing the venue, hands on
Faculty member 7	Internships
	Fashion Show

Three of the faculty specifically mentioned group work, and 3 mentioned "hands on". The three that said "hands on" were referring to the Entertainment Management concentration within the School of Management. This concentration utilizes a classroom that doubles as a venue where both simulated and actual events are produced, hence the "hands on" responses. One other faculty member cited the fashion show produced by students as well as the required internships. Faculty member 2 uses simulation games to provide application experience. Faculty member 1 mentioned DECA, formerly Delta Epsilon Chi, an organization that promotes business case study competition among member schools. All of the faculty members interviewed had designed opportunities to apply leadership content knowledge into their curriculum.

Finding 7.0. The final interview question asked faculty about other elements of the college experience that prepare students for leadership. The intent was to uncover experiences outside of the formal curriculum. Table 13 displays the responses and frequencies from both groups.

Table 13

Students' responses to research question 4 and faculty responses to research question 7

Students	Faculty
DECA	DECA
3	3
The venue	MEISA
1	2
MEISA	Fashion Show
1	1
SGA	General Education
3	1
Peer mentor	SGA
1	1

RA	RA
1	1
Student ambassador	Habitat
1	1
Internships	Internships
2	3
Mass lodging	
1	

The student and faculty responses to this question differed from the earlier questions in that there was a great deal of agreement. Three of the faculty members mentioned DECA. Two of the faculty cited MEISA, the Music and Entertainment Industry Student Association, along with 1 faculty member that mentioned student government, or SGA. One of the SOM faculty said being a RA (dormitory resident assistant) was something that would prepare students for leadership. Three faculty cited internships as contributing to students' preparedness for leadership. All of the above faculty responses were also mentioned by students in Finding 4.0.

In addition to the aforementioned points of agreement, there were other elements of the college experience cited by one group and not the other. One member of the SOM faculty said that both the Fashion Show and general education were elements that should be included here, along with students' participation with Habitat for Humanity.

This final question, intended to elicit extra-curricular responses, provided the greatest area of agreement between faculty and students in the interview portion of this mixed-method case-study. Some of the replies could be considered curricular, but these curricular responses were included here by the researcher.

Summary of the Chapter

The quantitative portion of the study consisted of 44.7% of the school of management seniors (N=38) taking the SLPI. The resulting means for the five leadership practices found the school of management seniors scoring higher than Posner's much larger reference group in all areas. The more detailed results displayed in table 8 indicated areas of relative strength, as well as areas that may provide opportunities for curricular refinements.

Finding 1.0. Among the areas of strength in the broad leadership practices were *Inspire a Shared Vision* and *Challenge the Process*, although the SOM scored above Posner's group in the remaining 3 practices as well. Greater variability was seen in the sub-behaviors, with the strongest being question 8, *Helps others take risks,* 9, *Actively listens* and 19, *Supports decisions other people make.* There were some areas that could represent opportunities for curriculum revision. The lowest scoring areas included question 18, *Asks "What can we learn"*, question 30, *Creatively recognizes people*, question 25, *Celebrates accomplishments,* and question 15, *Provides support and appreciation.*

The qualitative portion of the study relied on interviews with 10 students and 7 members of the school of management faculty. It should be noted that the one faculty member responsible for teaching managerial leadership was unable to participate in the interviews.

Finding 2.0. The first question directed to the students asked: *How well prepared are you to meet potential employers' expectations of a candidate's leadership development?* All of the students affirmed that they believed they were prepared to meet or exceed those expectations. Responses included; very well, pretty well, better than before college, above and beyond, pretty prepared, I network with experienced people, as prepared as I can be, and pretty confident, I feel I can do it.

Finding 3.0.. The next interview question directed to the students asked; *what are your perceptions about the elements of the curriculum that contributed most to your leadership development?* The response cited most often was the course Managerial Leadership, cited by 5 of the 10 participants. Strategic Management, Organizational Behavior, and the Entertainment Practicum garnered 2 each.

Finding 4.0. The final student interview questions asked about other elements of the college experience that prepare students for leadership. In response, three students mentioned that the DECA case study competition team was an element of the college experience that helped to prepare students for leadership. One Student cited MEISA, the Music and Entertainment Industry Student Association. Three students mentioned the Student Government Association, while one said that being a RA (dormitory resident assistant) was something that would prepare students for leadership. Two students cited internships as contributing to students' preparedness for leadership.

Finding 5.0. Faculty responded to the inquiries related to the research question *How does the management curriculum, as reported by program faculty, help students acquire leadership content knowledge?* The interview questions addressed the acquisition of content knowledge in each of the five practices, prompting faculty to cite course titles where the curriculum provided the corresponding information.

Finding 5.a. Regarding the behavior Model the Way, faculty responses included 3 of the 8 citing Principles of Management as a course that teaches leadership. One faculty member cited Introduction to Business, while four entertainment management courses were specified by a single faculty member:

Entertainment Management, Events Management, Venue Management, and Concert Production. Strategic Management was cited on 1 occasion, by the program chair. The program chair also stated that content knowledge related to modeling the way is "woven throughout the curriculum".

Finding 5.b. When asked about the leadership practice Inspire a Shared Vision, Public Speaking was recalled by 1 faculty member. Negotiations, Event Management, Venue Management, Concert Production, and Textiles were each mentioned once by faculty.

Finding 5.c. In response to the question about the third leadership practice, Challenge the Process, 3 faculty members again cited Principles of Management. 2 faculty members mentioned the Entertainment Practicum, and the following were each mentioned once: Strategic Management, Events Management, Venue Management, and Concert Production.

Finding 5.d. Faculty responses to the interview question about Enable Others to Act included 2 for Principles of Management and 1 each for Events Management, Venue Management, and Concert Production.

Finding 5.e. Faculty responses to the question regarding the practice Encourage the Heart included 1 each for Principles of Management, Events Management, Venue Management, and Concert Production.

Included in the faculty responses were instructional strategyies that were intended to help students learn the content knowledge related to the 5 practices. Among the intra-course activities, four of the faculty members interviewed felt that the practice Model the Way was best demonstrated through case studies and like simulations. One faculty member stated that she believed it best to personally provide an example, or in other words, model the way herself. When responding to the question addressing Inspire a Shared Vision, 2 of the faculty interviewed mentioned group work, and one cited case studies. When answering the question regarding the practice Challenge the Process, one faculty member said that case studies were their preferred method of teaching this practice. The responses for instructional strategies that help teach the practice Enable Others to Act included 2 faculty members saying anything "hands on", and one that admonished that case studies were most effective. instructional strategies related to the practice Encourage the Heart included 2that replied "hands on", and one that said that working at the annual Fashion Show would teach this practice.

Finding 6.0. Faculty were asked, How does the management curriculum, as reported by program faculty, provide students with experiences to apply leadership content knowledge? Three of the faculty specifically mentioned group work, and 3 mentioned "hands on". One other faculty member cited the fashion show produced by students as well as the required internships. Faculty member 2 uses simulation games to provide application experience. Faculty member 1 mentioned DECA. All of the faculty interviewed had designed opportunities to apply leadership content knowledge into their curriculum.

Finding 7.0. The final interview question asked faculty about other elements of the college experience that prepare students for leadership. Three of the faculty members mentioned DECA. Two of the faculty cited MEISA, the Music and Entertainment Industry Student Association, along with 1 faculty member that mentioned student government, or SGA. One of the SOM faculty said being a RA (dormitory resident assistant) was something that would prepare students for leadership. Three faculty cited internships as contributing to students' preparedness for leadership. One member of the SOM faculty said that both the Fashion Show and general education were elements that should be included here, along with students' participation with Habitat for Humanity.

Chapter Five: Summary, Conclusions, and Recommendations

Introduction

This chapter presents a summary of the study, the conclusions, and a set of recommendations. The summary includes an overview of the problem, the conceptual framework, and the research questions, along with the design, methodology, and findings. The conclusions are based on the study's findings, as are a set of recommendations that focus on the prospects for future research and opportunities for application of the findings to educational leadership.

Statement of the Problem

The need for competent leaders in business and industry has grown with the increase of competitive pressures and the continuing trend toward globalization (Lang, 2001). At the same time, many studies, such as those described in chapter two, have determined that the development of students' leadership abilities is a desirable outcome of a business education. One of the primary purposes of a business program is leadership preparation. The students' readiness to demonstrate a fundamental level of ability as leaders is an important aspect of career preparation for business students. The businesses that will employ them will look to hire those that have learned enough leadership content to feel ready for initial employment.

Some previous research (Komives, Lucas, & McMahon, 2007) indicated that leadership development has long been a mission in higher education. It would follow that the processes used to teach leadership should be identified, and the outcomes correlated. One of the primary purposes of a business program is career preparation. Students' self-reports of their leadership practices as described by Kouzes and Posner (2002) provide a lens for examining the students' perceptions of their ability to apply leadership content. The students' ability to demonstrate a fundamental level of ability as leaders is an important aspect of career preparation for business students. The businesses that will employ them will look to hire those that satisfy their requirements.

Pfeffer (2009) observed that although there are many reasons why leadership development is important, in higher education assessment of leadership is rare. Moreover, he stated that in general, colleges and universities have failed to supply business and industry with adequately prepared leaders. He maintains that the core of the problem is a lack of assessment.

The intent of this study is to determine what elements of a four-year business program help first time job seekers meet employers' expectations for leadership abilities by examining the self-reported leadership behaviors and answers to questions about academic preparation of students at a four-year college in a northeastern state. The curriculum designers of the college have embedded leadership content in various courses. Faculty interviews will attempt to provide insight how instructors often pair the lessons in leadership theory with application exercises, usually in the form of simulations such as case studies. Interviews will also attempt to reveal any additional opportunities to apply leadership content exist outside of the classroom in activities such as student government and case study competition teams. Faculty will be asked to provide accounts of how students may also gain leadership application experience while serving the internships required for graduation. While there is clearly opportunity for leadership development during the course of the business student's education at the college, there has been no documented observations revealing how much these students know about leadership, or which specific courses or activities contributed most to their leadership development.

There is evidence in the literature (Komives, Lucas, & McMahon, 2007, Cavico & Mujtaba ,2010; NACE, 2010; Garvin and Datar, 2008) that suggests that employers expect that business school graduates that they consider for employment possess at least foundational leadership content knowledge combined with some application experience. The college in this study and probably many others as well, has no method currently in place to determine which courses or activities are most effective in fostering students' leadership development, and no systematic method to measure the students' self-perceptions of their leadership skills.

Without obtaining data on the outcomes of teaching leadership, there is no way to be sure that business programs are serving the needs of students and the businesses that will employ them. By administering the S-LPI, which serves as an example of an application of leadership content, to seniors in the business program, it will be possible to determine students' perceptions of their leadership development. Additionally, this study revealed through student interviews what elements of the management program are perceived by students to teach leadership content, and students' perceptions of what elements provide opportunities for application of the content. By conducting faculty interviews this study also gathered faculty perceptions of the curricular elements intended to teach leadership, and provided insights into what leadership content these seniors know. This study's findings can serve as a guide to future program refinements, with the goal of increasing students' leadership knowledge and application abilities.

Conceptual Framework

The conceptual framework that guided this study is derived from Kouzes and Posner's (2002) five practices of exemplary leadership. For nearly three decades, Kouzes and Posner (2002) have compiled findings from their research on the dynamic process of leadership. Through case analyses and survey questionnaires, they uncovered five practices of exemplary Leadership that were "common to personal-best leadership experiences" (p. 13). These practices are (a) Model the Way, (b) Inspire a Shared Vision, (c) Challenge the Process, (d) Enable Others to Act, and (e) Encourage the Heart.

Research Questions

The following research questions guided this study.

Research question 1.   What are business students' self-reports about their leadership behaviors as articulated by Kouzes and Posner and measured by the S-LPI (Kouzes & Posner, 2002).

Research question 1a.   What are business students' self-reports about the leadership behavior Model the Way.

Research question 1b.   What are business students' self-reports about the leadership behavior Inspire a Shared Vision.

Research question 1c.   What are the business students' self-reports about the leadership behavior Challenge the Process.

Research question 1d.   What are business students' self-reports about the leadership behavior Enable Others to Act.

Research question 1e.   What are business students' self-reports about the leadership behavior Encourage the Heart.

Research question 2.   What are business students' self-reports about their preparedness to meet potential employers' expectations of a candidate's leadership development?

Research question 3.   What are business students' perceptions about the elements of the curriculum that contributed most to their leadership development?

Research question 4. What are business students' perceptions about other elements of the college experience that may prepare them for leadership?

Research question 5. How does the management curriculum, as reported by program faculty, help students acquire leadership content knowledge?

Research question 6. How does the management curriculum, as reported by program faculty, provide students with experiences to apply leadership content knowledge?

Research question 7. Are there any other elements of the college experience that may prepare students for leadership?

Design of the Study

This study applied a single case study design. The purpose of the study was to describe how students and faculty perceive the college's management program develops the students' leadership knowledge and skills. This study also described how the elements of the program's curriculum are intended to help students meet employers' expectations for leadership abilities in the candidates they consider for employment.

Yin (2009) said "that case studies are the preferred method when (a) "how" or "why" questions are being posed, (b) the investigator has little control over events, and (c) the focus is on a contemporary phenomenon within a real-life context"(p. 2). All of these conditions were true in this case, and the researcher was not going to intervene in any way with the contemporary phenomenon being studied. The phenomenon of a business program preparing students in terms of leadership development to meet employers' expectations is a contemporary, increasingly important aspect of a business student's academic preparation.

In this case study the researcher collected evidence from individuals using three separate data collection tools. The three different instruments that were utilized were a student interview guide, a faculty interview guide, and a survey. Thus, complementary lines of inquiry were used in this study to help us understand strategies used in this business program to help students develop their leadership skills.

The SLPI was the survey instrument used, and it provided baseline information about the students' self perceptions of their leadership development. Forty four percent of the seniors in the School of Management participated, with the results then compared to a larger reference group of college students.

Ten students randomly selected from the SLPI group were interviewed along with 7 of the eight full-time faculty members in the School of Management. The intent of the interviews was to reveal where and how faculty designed curriculum to teach leadership, and where did students report that they learned about leadership and how prepared they felt they were for initial employment in terms of their leadership abilities.

Participants

Currently, the participating college in this study has a total enrollment of 753 students; 199 men and 554 women. The School of Management has 205 students enrolled in the Bachelor of Science in Management program. These enrolled students have the options of concentrations in Management, Marketing, Hospitality Management, and Entertainment Management, and Fashion Merchandizing. The School of Management has 8 full-time faculty members combined with a list of adjunct instructors that can be changed to reflect variations in enrollment. The 8 full-time faculty members are responsible for creation and revision of the curricula for the courses that they teach. The full-time faculty is comprised of 3 men and 5 women. Seven of the 8 of the full-time faculty members within the school of management agreed to be interviewed regarding the elements of their curricula intended to foster leadership development among students.

Data Collection Activities

This single case study was conducted in three phases. First, 38 of the 85 students in their final year agreed to complete the SLPI (Kouzes & Posner, 2002). Then, a group of 10 students, randomly selected from the SLPI group were interviewed about their self perceptions of their leadership development, specifically the extent to which the management curriculum has assisted in their leadership development. Second, the full time faculty members from the School of Management at the small private college in a northeastern state were interviewed about the elements of the curriculum intended to foster students' leadership development. The student and faculty interviews were designed by the researcher, reviewed by the researcher's advisor and pilot tested.

Data Analysis

Yin (2009) wrote of four general strategies for data analysis in case studies. The third of these he called *Using both qualitative and quantitative data* (p. 132). The author wrote of case studies with substantial amounts of quantitative data subjected to statistical analysis, that if qualitative data remains "central to the entire case study, you will have successfully followed a strong analytic strategy" (p. 132). Such was the goal of the data analysis in this study. The student SLPI results were loaded into Excel, which generated statistics including frequencies, means, and standard deviations. The qualitative data generated by both the student and faculty interviews were extracted from the transcriptions of the interviews and the subsequent open-coding.

Summary of Results

Summary of results for Primary Research Question 1

The primary research question was: What are business students' self-reports about their leadership behaviors as articulated by Kouzes and Posner and measured by the S-LPI (Kouzes & Posner, 2002).

Finding 1.0: Among the areas of strength in the broad leadership practices were *Inspire a Shared Vision* and *Challenge the Process*, although the SOM scored above Posner's group in the remaining 3 practices as well. Greater variability was seen in the sub-behaviors, with the strongest being question 8, *Helps others take risks,* 9, *Actively listens* and 19, *Supports decisions other people make.* There were some areas that could represent opportunities for curriculum revision. The lowest scoring areas included question 18, *Asks "What can we learn",* question 30, *Creatively recognizes people,* question 25, *Celebrates accomplishments,* and question 15, *Provides support and appreciation.*

Summary of results for Primary Research Question 2

Research question 2 was: What are business students' self-reports of their preparedness to meet potential employers' expectations of a candidate's leadership development?

Finding 2,0: The first question directed to the students asked: *How well prepared are you to meet potential employers' expectations of a candidate's leadership development?* All of the students affirmed that they believed they were prepared to meet or exceed those expectations. Responses included; very well, pretty well, better than before college, above and beyond, pretty prepared, I network with experienced people, as prepared as I can be, and pretty confident, I feel I can do it.

Summary of results for Primary Research Question 3

Research question 3 was: What are business students' perceptions of the elements of the curriculum that contributed most to their leadership development?

Finding 3.0: The next interview question directed to the students asked; *what are your perceptions about the elements of the curriculum that contributed most to your leadership development?* The response cited most often was the course Managerial Leadership, cited by 5 of the 10 participants. Strategic Management, Organizational Behavior, and the Entertainment Practicum garnered 2 each. Among the intra-course activities mentioned, group work was the most common response.

Summary of results for Primary Research Question 4

Research question 4 was: What are business students' perceptions of other elements of the college experience that may prepare them for leadership?

Finding 4.0: The final student interview questions asked about other elements of the college experience that prepare students for leadership. In response, three students mentioned that the DECA case study competition team was an element of the college experience that helped to prepare students for leadership. One Student cited MEISA, the Music and Entertainment Industry Student Association. Three students mentioned the Student Government Association, while one said that being a RA (dormitory resident assistant) was something that would prepare students for leadership. Two students cited internships as contributing to students' preparedness for leadership.

Summary of results for Primary Research Question 5

Research question 5 was: How does the management curriculum, as reported by program faculty, help students acquire leadership content knowledge?

Finding 5.0: Faculty responded to the inquiries related to the research question *How does the management curriculum, as reported by program faculty, help students acquire leadership content knowledge?* The interview questions addressed the acquisition of content knowledge in each of the five practices, prompting faculty to cite course titles where the curriculum provided the corresponding information.

Summary of results for Primary Research Question 6:

Research question 6 was: How does the management curriculum, as reported by program faculty, provide students with experiences to apply leadership content knowledge?

Finding 6.0: . Faculty were asked, How does the management curriculum, as reported by program faculty, provide students with experiences to apply leadership content knowledge? Three of the faculty specifically mentioned group work, and 3 mentioned "hands on". One other faculty member cited the fashion show produced by students as well as the required internships. Faculty member 2 uses simulation games to provide application experience. Faculty member 1 mentioned DECA. All of the faculty interviewed had designed opportunities to apply leadership content knowledge into their curriculum.

Summary of results for Primary Research Question 7

Research question 7 was: Are there any other elements of the college experience that may prepare students for leadership?

Finding 7.0: The final interview question asked faculty about other elements of the college experience that prepare students for leadership. Three of the faculty members mentioned DECA. Two of the faculty cited MEISA, the Music and Entertainment Industry Student Association, along with 1 faculty member that mentioned student government, or SGA. One of the SOM faculty said being a RA (dormitory resident assistant) was something that would prepare students for leadership. Three faculty cited internships as contributing to students' preparedness for leadership. One member of the SOM faculty said that both the Fashion Show and general education were elements that should be included here, along with students' participation with Habitat for Humanity.

Conclusions and Recommendations

The conclusions and recommendations from this study are presented below. Each conclusion is followed by a recommendation for practice and a recommendation for future research based on that conclusion.

Conclusion 1

Students in their final year at the participating school of management reported opportunities to perform most of the leadership behaviors identified by Kouzes and Posner (2002).

The overall results of the SLPI indicated that reports by the School of Management students in this study compare favorably with the larger group of college students compiled by Posner (2010). A closer examination revealed that the lowest scoring responses to questions described students' self perceptions about Enabling Others to Act and Encouraging the Heart. These findings represent opportunities for curriculum refinements similar to the SLPI-based refinements of Judge (2005) at the University of Tennessee MBA program.

Recommendation for practice derived from Conclusion 1

To strengthen the students' self perceptions of their leadership preparedness, application simulations such as case studies and simulations that demonstrate the benefits of maintaining effort and keeping the focus on the strategic goals, even in the face of tactical challenges, could prove beneficial.

Recommendation for research derived from Conclusion 1

Secondary analysis of the SLPI results in other studies using the instrument may help to determine if the conclusions of this study are indicative of a broader trend. If any such trend exists, it could be worthwhile to determine if it is more prevalent at smaller, career-focused programs such as the one in this study, or ubiquitous across diverse programs.

Conclusion 2

The students in this study all reported their leadership abilities were sufficiently developed to meet or exceed potential employers' expectations. In terms of self-efficacy, the School of Management appears to successfully develope student confidence.

The unanimous affirmation of preparedness by the students interviewed indicated their self-efficacy was strong enough to satisfy or exceed employers' expectations. The researcher was unable to locate another finding in the literature that replicates this outcome.

Recommendation for practice derived from Conclusion 2

Efforts to enhance students' confidence at the participating school of management should not be a priority at the current time.

Recommendation for research derived from Conclusion 2

Based on the results of this study, several follow-up studies seem warranted regarding students' abilities to meet employers' expectations. Interviews of a larger sample of students should be conducted. Studies similar to this one, but conducted at other institutions, may be valuable. Longitudinal interviews with the students that participated in this study, following several years of employment, should be conducted.

Conclusion 3

Students reported superior recall of content knowledge that was delivered during the program via application exercises rather than by passive learning strategies such as lecture.

While learning by doing is effective, without broader content knowledge learning by application can become too narrow (Joyce, 2012). This finding is consistent with other studies that cited the benefits of experiential education (Hunt and Weintraub, 2004; Godson, 2007).

Recommendation for practice derived from Conclusion 3

If students' self-perceptions of leadership preparedness are important to the participating School of Management than the decision to add a course dedicated to leadership studies is affirmed. While many elements of the curriculum can and do contribute to students' understanding of the subject, no other course was recalled as frequently y students. Similar business programs may wish to consider the addition to their respective curricula. As mentioned earlier in this study, MBA programs along with larger, more traditional Baccalaureate business programs have frequently included this component. It seems likely that other schools similar in size and focus to the participating school of mangement may also benefit from the strategy.

Group work is beneficial in teaching leadership, and should be included in any course where it is practical to do so. In addition to providing benefits to students' leadership development, it is one of Marzano's (2009) High Yield Strategies for differentiating instruction. Moreover, use of group work can be part of the approach outlined by Heames and Service (2003) described previously in chapter 2.

Recommendation for research derived from Conclusion 3

Studies at similar career focused business programs might also gather data indicating the relative level of students' self-perceptions of their leadership development. The SLPI, or a similar instrument, might furnish the baseline data which can be supplemented by qualitative methods that expand the investigators understanding. Furthermore, the qualitative aspects might yield valuable insights into group work and other instructional strategies. Curricular refinements could then be contemplated.

Conclusions 4 and 7

While students' responses were consistent with reports that active learning within the classroom provided acquisition of content knowledge, students indicated that extra-curricular activities involving leadership were especially valued in fostering content learning.

The list generated by faculty was very similar to the list from the students. These extra-curricular activities are often seen as amenities to the formal program, but in fact they can also be essential to students' career preparation.

The faculty at the participating school should consider these extra-curricular activities as opportunities to extend and correlate with the curriculum being delivered in the program's various courses. The leadership applications provided by extra-curricular activities, if linked to the existing course content, can increase student recall and understanding of effective leadership behaviors.

The current array of extra-curricular activities available at the participating school provide numerous opportunities for students to gain experience with applications of leadership knowledge.

Recommendation for practice derived from Conclusion 4 and 7

Conclusion 4 suggests that the participating school of management should look for ways to correlate the classroom content with the extra-curricular leadership activities within the school. Management programs in other schools may also benefit from correlating curricular and extra-curricular content activities involving leadership.

Similarly in conclusion 7, the School of Management in this study should promote and encourage the extra-curricular activities available at this time. Generally low cost, the School of Management should maintain the current assortment of extra-curricular activities, while being receptive to the possibility of adding new ones. Benchmarking other small, career focused colleges may provide additional ideas that could provide similar benefits to the students that participate in them. Other colleges may wish to review their offerings and revise accordingly.

Recommendation for research derived from Conclusions 4 and 7

Studies should be undertaken tracking the effects of extra-curricular activities on students' self perceptions of their leadership preparedness. Diverse settings and a broad range of student demographics should be components of such studies.

Moreover, conclusion 7 maintains that research may include the variety of extra-curricular activities available on college campuses, and the benefits derived from them. An inquiry into who at these colleges is usually responsible for implementation. A recent study by Kezar (2011) indicated that it is often a bottom-up member of the staff, someone outside of the formal, top-down authority structure. By examining these topics at diverse locations we may gain a better understanding of the intrinsic value of extra-curricular activities in leadership development and elsewhere.

Conclusion 5

Faculty in the participating school of management has designed into many courses the opportunities for learning leadership content knowledge.

Moreover, too often, students were unable to specifically report on these opportunities for learning leadership content knowledge.

Recommendation for practice derived from Conclusion 5

The participating program's freshman course, Management, should be revised. This study revealed that the majority of instructors believe this course provides leadership content knowledge, and revision is needed if the educational outcomes are to be closer to faculty intentions. Techniques described by Heames and Service (2003) may prove effective. An example of this includes what the authors call *Class Objectives,* where the teacher to lists the lessons learning objectives on the board, and the students lead their own discussion exploring the objectives.

Recommendation for research derived from Conclusion 5

This study should be replicated following the implementation of the curriculum revision to assess the impacts of those revisions.

Conclusion 6

All of the faculty members interviewed in this study had designed into the curriculum opportunities for students to apply leadership content knowledge.

The methods included both actual and simulated activities. This is vital to building confidence, since students will rely on what they learned from their limited experience when they assume leadership roles early in their careers. The application opportunities provided by faculty closely mirror the list generated by students when asked where they learned about leadership.

Recommendation for practice derived from Conclusion 6

While teaching leadership content knowledge provides the foundational knowledge students will need, applications provide the memorable lessons that students recall. Applications should be included in the curriculum where possible.

Recommendation for research derived from Conclusion 6

Researchers may wish to determine which applications have the greatest impact on students' leadership development. Possible approaches could be to compare actual leadership activities such as managing the venue, leading a work group at the fashion show, or being involved in student government with simulations such as case studies and games that replicate the activities of actual leaders. These and other similar topics could also be studied in diverse settings.

Final Thoughts

This study clearly demonstrated the importance of providing opportunities for students to practice the leadership behaviors as described by Kouzes and Posner (2002). Based on the study's findings, students readily recall the opportunities to apply the content knowledge, while having difficulty remembering which courses contained leadership curriculum. Moreover, students frequently cited instructional strategies that provided opportunities to apply leadership content knowledge, even in otherwise unrelated courses and extra-curricular activities. Other investigators may wish to examine other elements of the college experience at diverse locations, attempting to reveal further activities that have value in teaching about leadership.

The balance between leadership content knowledge and application at the participating school of management should be maintained, and where possible enhanced. At their best such lessons are both memorable and sufficiently broad enough to facilitate a level of self-efficacy and ability in graduates to satisfy the needs of prospective employers.

The SLPI, as used in this study, can provide direction for curriculum revisions. By addressing deficiencies, programs and schools of business can strive for continuous improvements in their students' leadership development. Future researchers may wish to examine other methods of guiding curriculum revisions.

The need for competent leaders in business continues to grow, and business schools and programs must prepare students to assume the emerging leadership roles. Through continuous improvements to its leadership curricula, higher education can attempt to meet this expanding need.

References

Anderson, R. (2006). The Leadership Circle Profile: breakthrough leadership
105emphis105nt technology. Industrial and Commercial
Training, 38(4), 175-184. Retrieved March 27, 2011, from ABI/INFORM
Global. (Document ID: 1073404531).

Avolio, B., Bass, B., & Jung, D. (1999, December). Re-examining the components
of transformational and transactional leadership using the multifactor
leadership questionnaire. *Journal of Occupational and Organizational
Psychology, 72*(4), 441-463.

Burns, J. (1978). The power of leadership. *Leadership.* New York: Harper and
Row.

Buzash, M.D. (1994). Success of two-week intensive in program in French for
superior high school students on a university campus. Paper presented at the
Annual Meeting of the Central State conference on the Teaching of Foreign
Languages, Kansas City, MO. (ERIC Document Reproduction Service No.
ED 403 740).

Buss, D. (2001, December). When managing isn't enough: Nine ways to develop
the leaders you need. *Workforce, 80*(12), 44-48.

Caskey, S. (1994). Learning outcomes in intensive courses. *The journal of
continuing higher education,* (42), 23-27.

Cavico, F., & Mujtaba, B. (2010, January). As assessment of business schools'
student retention, accreditation, and faculty scholarship challenges.
Contemporary Issues in education, 3(1), 107-119.

Daniel, E. (2000). A review of time-shortened courses across disciplines. *College
student journal,* (34), 298-309.

Doh, J. (2003). Can leadership be taught? Perspectives from management educators. *Academy of management learning & education, 2*(1), 54-67.

Drew, Glenys M. (2006) Balancing academic advancement with business effectiveness?

The dual role for senior university leaders. *International Journal of Knowledge, Culture*

and Change Management, 6(4). pp. 117-125.

In. Retrieved October 17, 2010, from Harvard Business School Newsroom: http://www.hbs.edu/news/releases/svmp.html

Garvin, D., & Datar, S. (2008, October 14). *Business education in the 21st century.* [Breakout session]. Retrieved February 6, 2010, from Harvard Business School: The Business Summit: http:www.hbs.edu/centennial/businesssummit/business-society/business-education-in-the-21st-century-1.html

Godson, N. (2007). Note to business schools: Practice what you teach. *Baylor Business Review, 25*(2), 48-50.

Henebry, K. (1997). The impact of class schedule on student performance in a financial management course. *Journal of education for business,* (73), 114-120.

Hunt, J., & Weintraub, J. (2004). Learning developmental coching. *Journal of Management Education*, 28(1), 39-61. Retrieved July 27, 2011, from ABI/INFORM Global. (Document ID: 533426231).

Judge, W. (2005, April). Adventures in creating an outdoor leadership challenge course for an

eMBA program. *Journal of Management Education, 29*(2), 284-301.

Kegan, R. (1994), In Over Our Heads: The Mental Demands of Modern Life,
   Harvard University Press, Cambridge, MA.

Kenary, J. (2010). Service learning experience and undergraduate leadership
   behaviors: An action research case study. Ed.D. dissertation, University of
   Hartford, United States – Connecticut. Retrieved April 13, 2010, from
   Dissertations & Theses @ University of Hartford. (Publication No. AAT
   3387874).

Kezar, A., Bertram Gallant, T., & Lester, J. (2011). Everyday people making a
   difference on college campuses: the tempered grassroots leadership tactics of
   faculty and staff. *Studies In Higher Education, 36*(2), 129-151.

Komives, S., Lucas, N., & McMahon, T. (2007). *Exploring leadership:For college
   students who want to make a difference* (2nd ed.). San Francisco: Jossey-
   Bass.

Kouzes, J. M., & Posner, B. Z. (1995). *The Leadership Challenge.* 989 Market
   Street, San Francisco: Jossey-Bass.

Lasker, M., Donnelly, J. and Weathersby, R. (1975). Even on Sunday: An
   approach to teaching intensive courses for adults. *Harvard Graduate School
   Education Association Bulletin.* 19, 611.

Marzano, Robert J. (2009). Setting the Record STRAIGHT on "High-Yield"
Strategies. *Phi   Delta   Kappan.* 91(1), 30-37.

Morrison, J. (2003). Leadership is our business. *Journal of education for business,
   79*(1), 6-10.

Murdock, J., & Brammer, C. (2011). A Successful Model of Leadership Development for Community Practice Physicians. *Physician Executive*, 37(2), 52-54,56. Retrieved August 5, 2011, from ABI/INFORM Global. (Document ID: 2297623431).

Naceweb. [Knowledge Center]. (2010, January). Retrieved February 6, 2010, from NACEWeb: http://naceweb.org/

Nixon, R.O. (1996). A source document on accelerated courses and programs at accredited two & four year colleges and universities. (ERIC Document Reproduction Service No. ED 399 827).

N/A. (June, 1988). *Hood: answers in action* (ED 299 845, pp. 1-37). Frederick, Maryland: Hood College.

Petrowsky, M. C. (1996). The two week summer macroeconomics course: Success or failure? (ERIC Document Reproduction Service No. ED 396779).

Pfeffer, J. (2009). Leadership development in business schools: an agenda for change.

Popper, M., & Lipshitz, R. (1993). Putting leadership theory to work: A conceptual framework for theory-based leadership development. *Leadership & Organization Development Journal, 14*(7), 23-28.

Posner, B. (2004, July). A leadership development Instrument for Students: Updated. *Journal of College Student Development, 45*(4), 443-457.

Posner, B. (2009, Sep). A longitudinal study examining changes in student's leadership behavior. *Journal of College Student Development, 50*(5), 551-563.

Reed, L., Vidaver-Cohen, D., & Colwell, S.. (2011). A New Scale to Measure

Executive Servant Leadership: Development, Analysis, and Implications for Research. *Journal of Business Ethics*, 101(3), 415-434. Retrieved August 16, 2011, from ABI/INFORM Global. (Document ID: 2399065361).

Robbins, C., Bradley, E., Spicer, M., & Mecklenburg, G. (2008, May). Developing leadership in healthcare administration: A competency assessment tool/practitioner application. *Journal of Healthcare Management, 46*(3), 188-203.

Rubin, H. J., & Rubin, I. S. (2005). *Qualitative interviewing: The art of hearing data* (2nd ed.). Thousand Oaks, CA: Sage.

Smith, J.P. (1988). Effects of intensive college sources on student cognitive achievement, academic standards, student attitudes, and faculty attitudes. Doctoral dissertation, University of Southern California. Dissertation Abstracts International. 49, 746.

Taylor, R. (2007). Going the extra MILE: The 109emphis institute for leadership education leadership mentoring program. *Business Perspectives, 18*(4), 34-38.

University of Minnesota. (2010). Interviewing for Jobs & Internships: Qualities Employers Look for. In *University of Minnesota college of liberal arts career and community learning center interviewing guide.* Retrieved February 6, 2010, from University of Minnesota Career and Community Learning Center Interviewing Guide: http://www.cclc.umn.edu

Waechter, R.F. (1967). A comparison of achievement and retention by college junior students in   an earth science course after learning under massed and spaced conditions. Doctoral dissertation, Pennsylvania State University, 1967). Dissertation Abstracts International. 27, 11-A

Wolverton, M. (2006). Three Georgias in Atlanta :Lessons from business schools about finding your identity. *The International Journal of Educational Management*, 20(7), 507-519. Retrieved March 8, 2010, from ABI/INFORM Global. (Document ID: 1143400691).

Yin, R. (2009). *Case study research design and methods.* Thousand Oaks, California: Sage, Inc.

Appendix A

Informed Consent

Leadership Development: Self-Rating Scale

The purpose of study is to describe how students and faculty perceive the business program at a small northeastern college develops students' leadership skills. This self-rating scale, the Student Leadership Practices Inventory (Kouzes and Posner, 2002), is intended to gauge your perceptions about how elements of the college experience have helped you develop various leadership behaviors as part of your preparation for initial employment. Knowing such information may help you identify those areas of strength that can be used in your future leadership roles, and those that may need to be enhanced in various ways.

- You must be 18 years or older to participate in this survey.
- Completing the survey is voluntary and will not affect your grade in any course.
- You may choose not to complete the survey. Simply exit and log-off
- You may withdraw your participation at any time.
- You may skip questions.
- Risks of participation in the survey are not greater, considering probability and magnitude, than those ordinarily encountered in daily life.
- It will take you about **20 minutes** to complete the survey.
- By participating in this study, you may add to existing the knowledge base on how undergraduate students develop their leadership abilities.
- Information will be used in presentations and publications.
- Your name will not be associated with your answers.
- All your answers will be grouped with the answers of others.

- The data will not be coded in any identifiable way.
- All survey data will be reported in aggregate.
- All survey responses will be stored in a locked file cabinet.
- All survey responses will be destroyed upon completion of the study.
- If you have any questions about your rights as a research subject, please contact the University of Hartford Human Subjects Committee (HSC) at 860.768.4310. The HSC is a group of people that reviews research studies and protects the rights of people involved in research.

By signing below, you acknowledge that you have been informed about and consent to

be a participant in the study described above. Make sure that your questions are answered to your

satisfaction before signing. You are entitled to retain a copy of this consent agreement.

_____   _____

Study Participant Signature   Date

Thank you for participating. If you have any questions about this survey, you may contact:

William K. Vasbinder

Professor

School of Management, Bay State College

Phone: 617-217-9305

Email: wvasbinder@baystate.edu

Donn Weinholtz, Ph.D.

Chair – Dept. of Educational Leadership

Interim Chair – Dept. of Nursing

University of Hartford

Phone: 860-768-4186

Appendix B

Informed Consent
Leadership Development: Student and Faculty Interviews

The purpose of study is to describe how students and faculty perceive the business program at a small northeastern college develops students' leadership skills. These interviews are intended to gauge your perceptions about how elements of the college experience have helped students develop various leadership behaviors as part of their preparation for initial employment.

- You must be 18 years or older to participate in this interview.
- Completing the interview is voluntary and will not affect your grade in any course.
- You may choose not to complete the interview. Simply inform the interviewer that you do not wish to continue.
- You may withdraw at any time.
- You may skip questions.
- Risks of participation in the interview are not greater, considering probability and magnitude, than those ordinarily encountered in daily life.
- It will take you about **30 minutes** to complete the interview.
- By participating in this study, you may add to existing the knowledge base on how undergraduate students develop their leadership abilities.
- Information will be used in presentations and publications.
- Your name will not be associated with your responses.
- The interview will be audio-taped and transcribed.
- All your responses will be grouped with the responses of others.

- The data will not be coded in any identifiable way.
- All data will be reported in aggregate.
- All interview responses will be stored in a locked file cabinet.
- All survey responses will be destroyed upon completion of the study.
- If you have any questions about your rights as a research subject, please contact the University of Hartford Human Subjects Committee (HSC) at 860.768.4310. The HSC is a group of people that reviews research studies and protects the rights of people involved in research.

By signing below, you acknowledge that you have been informed about and consent to

be a participant in the study described above. Make sure that your questions are answered to your

satisfaction before signing. You are entitled to retain a copy of this consent agreement.

_____   _____

Study Participant Signature   Date

Thank you for participating. If you have any questions about this interview, you may contact:

William K. Vasbinder

Professor

School of Management, Bay State College

Phone: 617-217-9305

Email: wvasbinder@baystate.edu

Donn Weinholtz, Ph.D.

Chair – Dept. of Educational Leadership

Interim Chair – Dept. of Nursing

University of Hartford

Phone: 860-768-4186

Appendix C

Dr. Monica Hardesty, Chair

Human Subjects Committee

The University of Hartford

200 Bloomfield Avenue

West Hartford, CT 06117

Re: Research approval for William Vasbinder

Dr. Hardesty:

Professor William Vasbinder has presented his research proposal to the Scholarly Activity Committee of the Faculty Senate and has received approval to conduct a series of surveys and interviews here at Bay State College, pending approval from the Human Subjects Committee at the University of Hartford. Professor Vasbinder intends to administer the SLPI and conduct follow-up interviews with students and faculty in the Business Department in order to determine the extent to which business-focused extracurricular activities as well as leadership-focused curriculum influence student leadership capabilities.

As his Department Chair and Chair of the Scholarly Activity Committee, I have discussed Professor Vasbinder's scholarship with him at length and I fully endorse his plan. His research is fully compliant with Bay State College policy regarding human subject research and he has my enthusiastic support to seek the approval from the HSC at the University of Hartford to begin the next phase of his doctoral scholarship.

If I may provide any additional information or clarify any of the policies of the College, please do not hesitate to contact me. I thank you in advance for your Committee's consideration of Professor Vasbinder's application.

Sincerely,

William S. Koehler, PhD.

Chair, Business Department, Dean, School of Management

Bay State College

437 Boylston St., Boston, MA 02116

(617) 217-9360 wkoehler@baystate.edu

Appendix D

Student Leadership Practices Survey

The Student LPI Self (Kouzes & Posner, 2002) is a 30-item assessment instrument that allows an individual Leader to self-measure the frequency of specific leadership behaviors on a 5-point scale. Responses to all 30 statements are required, using the number from the following scale that best applies to each statement presented.

1 – Rarely or Seldom
2 – Once in a While
3 – Sometimes
4 – Often
5 – Very Frequently or Almost Always

1. I set a personal example of what I expect from other people.
2. I look ahead and communicate about what I believe will affect us in the future.
3. I look around for ways to develop and challenge my skills and abilities.
4. I foster cooperative rather than competitive relationships among people I work with.
5. I praise people for a job well done.
6. I spend time and energy making sure that people in our organization adhere to the principles and standards we have agreed upon.

7. I describe to others in our organization what we should be capable of accomplishing.

8. I look for ways that others can try out new ideas and methods.

9. I actively listen to diverse points of view.

10. I encourage others as they work on activities and programs in our organization.

11. I follow through on the promises and commitments I make in this organization.

12. I talk with others about sharing a vision of how much better the organization could be in the future.

13. I keep current on events and activities that might affect our organization.

14. I treat others with dignity and respect.

15. I give people in our organization support and express appreciation for the contributions.

16. I find ways to get feedback about how my actions affect other people's performance.

17. I talk with others about how their own interests can be met by working toward a common goal.

18. When things do not go as we expected, I ask, "What can we learn from this experience?"

19. I support the decisions that other people in our organization make on their own.

20. I make it a point to publicly recognize people who show commitment to our values.

21. I build consensus on a agreed-upon set of values for our organization.

22. I am upbeat and positive when talking about what our organization aspires to accomplish.

23. I make sure that we set goals and make specific plans for the projects we undertake.

24. I give others a great deal of freedom and choice in deciding how to do their work.

25. I find ways for us to celebrate accomplishments.

26. I talk about the values and principles that guide my actions.

27. I speak with conviction about the higher purpose and meaning of what we are doing.

28. I take initiative in experimenting with the way we can do things in our organization.

29. I provide opportunities for others to take on leadership responsibilities.

30. I make sure that people in our organization are creatively recognized for their contributions.

Appendix E

Student Interview guide

Protocol

Introduction

Consent form

Point out phone numbers for Researcher, Research Advisor, and Human Subjects
Committee

Interview questions

Thank participant for contributing to research

Ask if participant has questions

Remind participant of the level of caution given to protect their anonymity

1. How well prepared are you to meet potential employers' expectations of a
    candidate's leadership development?

2. What are your perceptions of the elements of the curriculum that contributed
    most to their leadership development?

2.a. Which elements of the curriculum taught you about the leadership behavior
      Model the Way?

2.b. Which elements of the curriculum taught you about the leadership behavior
      Inspire a Shared Vision?

2.c. Which elements of the curriculum taught you about the leadership behavior
      Challenge the Process?

2.d. Which elements of the curriculum taught you about the leadership behavior
      Enable Others to Act?

2.e.   Which elements of the curriculum taught you about the leadership behavior Encourage the Heart

3.   What other elements of the college experience have prepared you for leadership?

Appendix F

Faculty Interview Guide

Protocol

Introduction

Consent form

Point out phone numbers for Researcher, Research Advisor, and Human Subjects
Committee

Interview questions

Thank participant for contributing to research

Ask if participant has questions

Remind participant of the level of caution given to protect their anonymity

5. a.   How does the management curriculum help students acquire leadership
content knowledge about the behavior Model the Way?

5.b.   How does the management curriculum help students acquire leadership
content knowledge about the behavior Inspire a Shared Vision?

5.c.   How does the management curriculum help students acquire leadership
content knowledge about the behavior Challenge the Process?

5.d.   How does the management curriculum help students acquire leadership
content knowledge about the behavior Enable Others to Act?

5.e.   How does the management curriculum help students acquire leadership
content knowledge about the behavior Encourage the Heart?

6.   How does the management curriculum provide students with experiences to
apply leadership content knowledge?

7.   Are there any other elements of the college experience that may prepare
students for leadership?

Printed by
Schaltungsdienst Lange o.H.G., Berlin